CLASSICAL STYLES IN MODERN ARCHITECTURE

FROM THE COLONNADE TO DISJUNCTURED SPACE

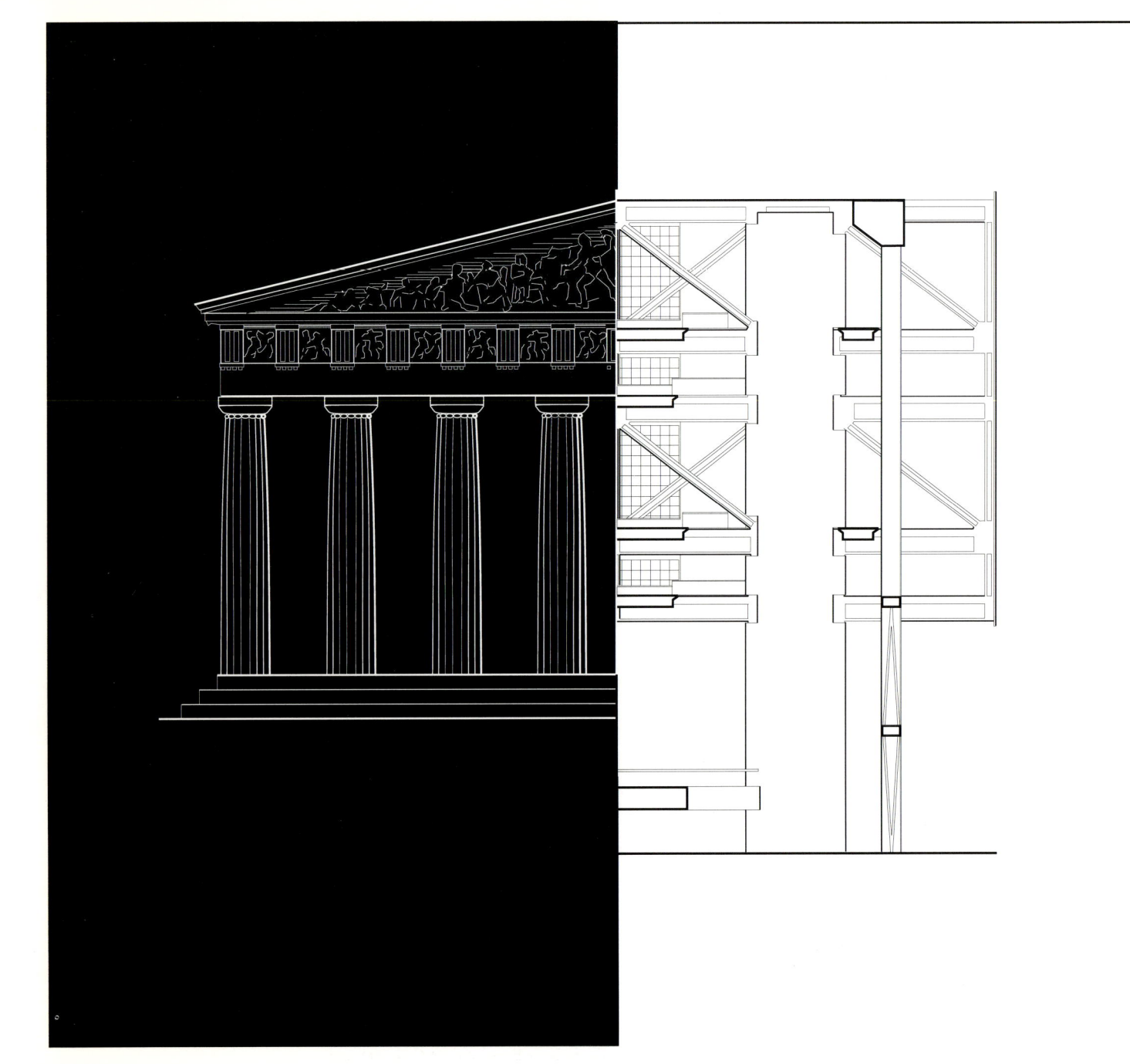

CLASSICAL STYLES IN MODERN ARCHITECTURE

FROM THE COLONNADE TO DISJUNCTURED SPACE

THOMAS DOREMUS

VAN NOSTRAND REINHOLD
An International Thomson Publishing Company

New York • London • Bonn • Boston • Detroit • Madrid • Melbourne • Mexico City
Paris • Singapore • Tokyo • Toronto • Albany NY • Belmont CA • Cincinnati OH

Copyright © 1994 by Van Nostrand Reinhold

 A division of International Thomson Publishing Inc.
ITP logo is a trademark under license.

Designed by Theo Coates Design
Cover illustration: Thomas Doremus
Interior illustrations: Theo Coates

Printed in the United States of America
For more information, contact:

Van Nostrand Reinhold
115 Fifth Avenue
New York, NY 10003

International Thomson Publishing
Berkshire House
168-173 High Holborn
London WC1V 7AA
England

Thomas Nelson Australia
102 Dodds Street
South Melbourne, Victoria 3205
Australia

Nelson Canada
1120 Birchmount Road
Scarborough, Ontario
M1K 5G4, Canada

International Thomson Publishing GmbH
Königswinterer Strasse 418
53227 Bonn
Germany

International Thomson Publishing Asia
221 Henderson Road
#05 10 Henderson Building
Singapore 0315

International Thomson Publishing Japan
Hirakawacho Kyowa Building, 3F
2-2-1 Hirakawa-cho, Chiyoda-ku
Tokyo 102
Japan

International Thomson Editores
Campos Eliseos 385, Piso 7
Col. Polanco
11560 Mexico D.F.
Mexico

All rights reserved. No part of this work covered by the copyright hereon may be reproduced or used in any form or by any means—graphic, electronic, or mechanical, including photocopying, recording, taping, or information storage and retrieval systems—without the written permission of the publisher.

1 2 3 4 5 6 7 8 9 10 ARCKP 01 00 99 98 97 96 95 94

Library of Congress Cataloging in Publication Data

Doremus, Thomas, 1946–
    Classical styles in modern architecture / Thomas L. Doremus.
      p. cm.
    Includes bibliographical references and index.
    ISBN 0-442-01666-2
    1. Neoclassicism (Architecture)—Influence. 2. Architecture, Modern.
      3. Architecture, Postmodern.   I. Title.
NA600.D67   1994
724'.6—dc20
                                            94-15137
                                              CIP

Dedication:

To my mother, Jeanne Hetherington Doremus, in love and respect.

Contents

	Introduction	2
1	History: From Oligarchy to Democracy	19
2	Technology: Abstraction of Knowledge	65
3	Culture: A Change of Scale	101
4	Form: From Static to Dynamic	137
	Notes	159
	Index	161

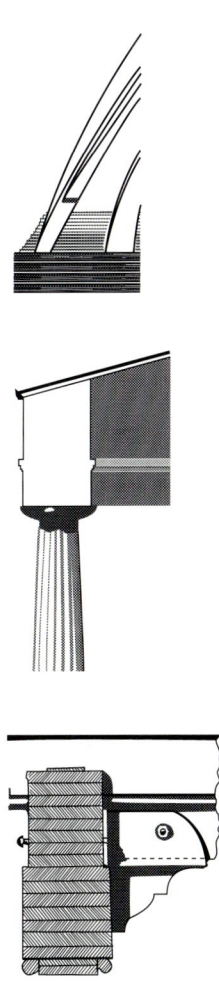
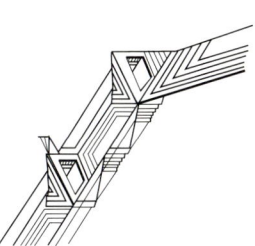
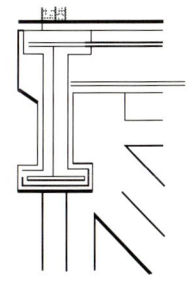

INTRODUCTION

The primary distinction in contemporary architecture is between what may be termed the classical and the modern. By "classical" is meant the collection of styles that aspire to the material shapes and forms of ancient Greek and Roman architecture and that have been codified through archaeological study and theoretical writing. The term "modern" has, in the twentieth century, come to denote a highly sophisticated, intellectual interpretation of architectural form based on human perception of three-dimensional space and emphasizing the technology of its construction.

The sharpness of this distinction has become apparent in two contemporary phenomena. First, the landmarks preservation movement gave rise to explosive controversies about style, most notably in Great Britain. Second, the sudden popularity in the 1980s of what attempted to be a composite style, dubbed "post-modernism," resulted in a series of major buildings whose appalling lack of architectural grace or coherence indicated some innate incompatibility between the classic and the modern, as usually defined.

Certainly, in studying the history of modern architecture, one becomes aware of an intentional break with the styles of the past by the great early modernists at the beginning of the twentieth century. The manifestation of an *avant-garde* in reaction to the control of the arts by the academies of the nineteenth century resulted in two distinct schools of thought in the arts. Especially in Europe, the rebuilding of urban areas destroyed during World War I demonstrated suddenly and shockingly the modern approach to design in contrast to traditional buildings in the classical style. In the Western hemisphere, particularly the United States, the change to modern styles was considerably more gradual.

The purpose of the present study is to examine the nature of the distinction between the classical and the modern and to demonstrate the connection of each to contemporary civilization, as major cities throughout the Western world retain many of their classical monuments and features. The persistence of traditional culture is in fact more

INTRODUCTION

striking in architecture than in other art forms because of the presence of older buildings in the midst of contemporary life. This study intends to present a more balanced view than the usual approach which sees the "International Style" as a challenge to revivalist architecture.

In America, the separation from ancient sources was extreme. No immediate monuments existed from which to copy. It was unusual for builders to have experienced in person the models they copied, and it can be said never to have been the case that such experience came before the influence of education. Precedents were set through written theory, through drawings, through teachers, through a vast industry of cultural hegemony. The result for most architects was an extreme abstraction from the immediate circumstances and conditions of nineteenth century life.

The loss of direct contact with culture has been mourned by many contemporary critics and theoreticians. Notable among these are Robert Venturi and Aldo Rossi, whose texts have been seminal for many architects and designers in the late twentieth century. But understanding and experiencing are two different processes. Through the vast enterprise of modern scholarship and its distribution system, the average undergraduate in classical studies probably knows more about Greek or Roman culture than those who lived it. In fact, it can be said to be characteristic of modern life that we know a lot about everything but experience comparatively little of it directly.

It is this intellectualization of culture, this abstraction, this enhanced ability to understand that has formulated both modernism and the contemporary version of classicism as well. One could almost say that classicism seeks to enlarge experience, whereas modernism seeks to explore the nature of abstraction. In 1947, John Summerson wrote:

Figure 1. Building near Times Square, New York. Grotesque combination of classical and modern motifs was endemic in American Architecture in the 1980s.

the time has probably come to ask not merely where this [modern] Architecture has come from but what it is. At the moment it can show no theoretical basis whatever, beyond a handful of generalisations borrowed . . . from Viollet-le-Duc, and a number of clichés which could be applied equally to most other styles of architecture.   1

In the late twentieth century, we are far from the "heroic" period of modernism. Iconoclasm is not very effective when the icons have been reduced to a surface pastiche:

In recent years a shift has taken place in the way we perceive reality, a shift so pervasive that it has radically altered basic assumptions about art and life. The shift is profound; it goes beyond the debate over modernism and post modernism and it increasingly affects the design of the buildings around us. Some, like myself, believe the shift mutilates and sells short what it pretends to elevate and embrace. It has instantly recognizable characteristics—an emphasis on surface gloss, on pastiche, on the use of familiar but bowdlerized elements from the history of design, on tenuous symbolism and synthetically created environments, a detachment from the problems and processes through which contemporary life and creative necessity are actively engaged. These attributes provide a dubious replacement for the rigorous and elegant synthesis of expression and utility that has always defined and enriched the best of the building art. This change in vision and values has brought irreversible changes in the understanding and practice of architecture today. The art of architecture as packaging or playacting is a notion whose time, alas, seems to have come.

I do not know just when we lost our sense of reality or interest in it, but at some point it was decided that the evidence of the built world around us was not compelling; that it was possible, permissible, and even desirable to substitute a more agreeable product. Once it was accepted that reality was disposable, its substance could be revised, manipulated, or abandoned. The devaluation of our cities and the structures in them that followed—essentially the abandonment of the richest and most revealing record of the human condition—has spread like a virus, invading and infecting architectural and urban standards in the most basic sense. The replacement of reality with selective fantasy has been led first by the preservation movement and then by a new, successful, and staggeringly profitable American phenomenon: the reinvention of the environment as themed entertainment. The process of substitution probably started in a serious way at Colonial Williamsburg, predating and preparing the way for the new world order of Disney Enterprises. Certainly it was in the restoration of Colonial Williamsburg that the studious fudging of facts received its scholarly imprimatur and history and place as themed artifact hit the big time.   2

Such a statement is only possible in the presence of a mature and self-conscious modern view that knows what it is about and what it is *not* about.

It can in fact be shown that modernism is not just another collection of visual motifs and structural details used in combination to create a palette of styles. Modernism assumes a different way of organizing the elements that go into a building—spatial and functional elements as well as structural—and it includes earlier architectural styles, primarily classicism and its multifarious manifestations. Modernism simultaneously incorporates and denies the classical ideal, and it is this very simultaneity that is its primary characteristic: an innate ambivalence that expresses irony rather than the classical ideal of harmony. All of the elements of contemporary architectonics such as enclosure, circulation, and structural support exemplify this essential difference.

For most of this century historians and critics have

explained the appearance of modern architecture through either functional or technological expression, finding in the changes in each a rich and relatively easily documented generator of modern form. At the end of the twentieth century, however, it seems questionable that these are essential determinants of a modern style.

A significant number of traditionally detailed buildings have always been under construction. Such buildings may not quite run the gamut of contemporary functions and techniques—traditionally detailed airport terminals are not easy to find—but they certainly represent most of the spectrum of building types. There does not appear to be any major restraint on the use of a building merely because it incorporates classical cornices and antique woodwork in a correct manner. Furthermore, the construction details of all contemporary buildings tend to be hidden beneath fireproof finishes and are flexible enough in nature to accommodate traditional proportions.

It is significant that one of the founders of American democracy was not only the third president of the United States but could be considered by the standards of his time a professional architect as well. Thomas Jefferson authored much of our Bill of Rights and Constitution. The laws that form the basis for the oldest continuous democratic government in the world derive largely from him and very few others. At the same time, almost alone among the signers, Jefferson sought to form the culture of the new nation as well, donating his personal library as the core collection of the Library of Congress. He also established a standard for the design of public buildings that would represent the ideals of democratic government.

> Whenever it is proposed to prepare plans for the Capitol, I should prefer the adoption of some one of the models of antiquity, which have had the approbation of thousands of years; and for the President's house, I should prefer the celebrated fronts of modern buildings, which have already received the approbation of all good judges. Such are the Galerie du Louvre, the Gardes meubles, and two fronts of the Hotel de Salm. 3

Thus, at the moment of the founding of the United States of America, there is a determination to pay attention to the classical tradition of Western architecture and at the same time a recognition of two distinct ways of doing that. Throughout the nineteenth century, architects either studied and refined the neoclassical ideal or sought alternative means of expression through stylistic experiments, such as the Gothic and Romanesque revival, that were associated in varying degrees with other historical styles.

Today it appears that the distinction between the modern and classical is sharper than ever. It makes sense, therefore, to seek an explanation for that distinction in the experience itself, to study what it is about a modern building that produces such an impression.

The self-conscious modernism recognizable today appeared around the turn of the twentieth century, most notably in the United States, in the work of Frank Lloyd Wright, but also in Europe. Simultaneously, the growth of neoclassicism was at its peak, as in the plans for the Columbian Exposition in Chicago of 1893; for the Capitol at Washington, D.C., by McKim, Mead & White; and for major urban renewal in New York, Chicago, Philadelphia, and elsewhere. Modernism, then, was born as a denial of the tradition of classicism.

The implications of this include the growth of democracy in the face of the waning imperial powers of Europe.

Even Jefferson's "modern" architecture grew during the revolutionary period in France. The imposition of European culture in the Western hemisphere initially destroyed native civilizations but retained their cultural elements to varying degrees. This, plus the importation of great numbers of slaves from Africa who brought with them traditions equally foreign to Western minds, eventually resulted in a rich stew of ideas that could not be resolved into a single, unified system. Obviously, the contradiction between the writing of the Bill of Rights and the existence of slavery was not resolved.

Thus, two modern answers can be given to the question of tradition as embodied in classical theory. One is a *denial* of the classical insistence on hierarchical order, on the subordination of part to whole, and the assertion of completeness of the classical object. The other is an *incorporation* of classically ordered elements into a larger modern object. Both of these approaches may be developed together in a modern style. Therefore, it may be said that the intention of the modern is to *include*, whereas the intention of the classical is always to *exclude*. The element of exclusion is essential to classical theory and allows it a coherence and rationality that modernism cannot achieve. Yet modernism includes by intention the classical system itself, but only in a critical way, as part of a problematic whole. For example, an urban space near Rittenhouse Square in Philadelphia displays characteristics of immediate interest to the modern eye, but the classical view would not consider it architecture at all. Indeed, the trace of a classically correct façade can be detected by the single course of light brick at the far edge of the main building. This side of the building, not visible in the photograph, has received attention by its architect that the rear has not.

The method by which modern architects have incorporated these distinctions into their designs is through the expression of *equivalent systems* of building elements. This can occur, as has been stated, at any or all of the levels of design: physical, functional, and cultural. It is proposed, in fact, that the richness of content of a modern work depends precisely on the extent and nature of the articulation of these systems and that it results in a uniquely modern experience of *disjunctured space*, a term defined later in the study.

The development of modern style, from this view, can be seen as a necessary and inevitable response to changes in social and cultural conditions that began occurring in developed countries in the nineteenth century and that have continued at an increasing rate throughout the twentieth. One result of this change is the permanent reduction of the classical ideal to a tra-

Figure 2. Building near Rittenhouse Square.

dition or memory, and its displacement as the primary mode of esthetic expression by modernism, which remains in its multifarious permutations the sole viable stylistic system today.

The purpose of this study is to provide a benchmark by which architectural works and projects may be measured to determine genuinely modern content. Stylistic variants may then be evaluated for their potential as modes of expression of modern content. The need for this arises from the peculiar circumstances of the development of modern architectural theory. At a particular moment in time—1930 to be exact—a view of modernism was established that, problematic though it has been for subsequent theory, is rarely challenged. This study seeks to pursue such a challenge in order to support much-needed clarity in contemporary discourse.

The Campidoglio and Lincoln Center

The codification of what has come to be known as the Modern Movement took place in 1930 when an exhibition of modern architecture was mounted at the Museum of Modern Art in New York. The catalogue for that exhibition was later published as a book, *The International Style*, by Henry-Russell Hitchcock and Philip Johnson. What was represented as modern architecture was really only one of the most prominent styles then current, and it was presented in a closed, stylistic way.

The greatest effect of this has been to fuse an image of "modern" into contemporary consciousness that does not adequately define the modern sensibility. One of the most prominent examples of this is the cultural complex at Lincoln Center in New York constructed in the 1950s and 1960s. It was meant to concentrate new cultural and educational facilities in an area filled with housing considered undesirable by contemporary city planners. The politics of this process are not part of this discussion except to point out that a great deal of (mostly private) money was spent on the project, and great profits were realized by speculators who held property adjacent to the Center. The style of the buildings was considered typical Modern Movement or International Style, but the organization and design of the public plaza and façades were based, of all places, on the Campidoglio in Rome as created by Michelangelo in the sixteenth century. When the designers of a twentieth century monument in the International Style decide to follow a Renaissance monument for inspiration, questions arise about the nature of modernism.

> The projects of Rossellino [at Pienza] and Michelangelo have similar devices: the regular plan, symmetrically organized about the entrance axis of the central building; the systematization of the entrance ways into the piazza, and the pavement pattern calculated to integrate the several buildings. 4

James Ackerman's comparison is a modern view of Renaissance architecture and can be applied as well to Lincoln Center. The references to Michelangelo's Campidoglio are overt: the quadrilateral plaza open on one side to the city, the two-story articulation, the matched structures on three sides, the public nature of plaza and buildings, the similarities in materials. Key to Ackerman's analysis is his citation of "a pattern calculated to integrate the several buildings." It is this impulse toward integration that is the kernel for the classical styles. What then is it that makes the Lincoln Center suite of buildings "modern"?

From the point of view of the International Style, the emphasis on the structure and the large expanses of glass determine these buildings to be modern. Whether the slim columns are quite the *pilotis* of Corbusier Revival is a moot question. However, the structural expression—a "giant

Figure 3. Campidoglio. Palazzo Nuovo. Michelangelo, ca. 1568.

INTRODUCTION

Figure 4. Lincoln Center. New York State Theater. Philip Johnson, 1964.

Figure 5. Campidoglio. Palazzo dei Senatori. Michelangelo, ca. 1568.

INTRODUCTION

Figure 6. Lincoln Center. Metropolitan Opera House. Harrison & Abramovitz, 1966.

order" of columns with a subordinate motif in the passageways at the lateral sides of the plaza—is a quotation of Michelangelo's seminal work in Rome. The giant order invented by Michelangelo there, in fact, is frequently cited as a defining characteristic of the High Renaissance and an essential precursor of the Baroque.

The transparency of the Lincoln Center lobbies may be claimed as a modern characteristic. There is certainly an opportunity for esthetic expression afforded by the technological development of glass walls. The twin ceremonial stair of the Metropolitan Opera House was derived from the Beaux-Arts Paris Opera but is also similar in configuration to the Capitol at Rome. When one takes into account the functional differences between the foyer of the Opera and the entrance of the Capitol, the former really serves as the forecourt of the Center, and the indoor/outdoor difference is more a question of climate and technological circumstance than of style. Glass rooms were not an option for Michelangelo.

But technological change by itself is not a sufficient distinction between major architectural styles. The Greeks of 600 B.C., the Romans of A.D. 100, the Italians of A.D. 1500, and the French of A.D. 1800 all built with different resources and technical knowledge, and it has always been an essential claim of classicism that it overrides such differences. If this is accepted, then modern construction techniques must be applicable to classicism as well. At Lincoln Center as on the Capitoline, symmetrical structures are expressed as two-story blocks, articulated in colonnaded bays and clad in travertine.

From the point of view of function, little distinction can be made. Both plazas are ceremonial public spaces with adjoining building façades designed primarily for this, rather than for specific internal use. The most appealing aspect of Lincoln Center is the way in which those attending performances can participate, through the large glass walls of the three lobbies, together in a great central space. To the degree that this space is sensed coherently, the exterior walls are made transparent and this could be said to be a modern experience rather than classical.

One is left with the classical vocabulary of proportion and detailing. Lincoln Center's structures are detailed in travertine like the Campidoglio, in this case cladding a supporting steel frame. Although there are arches and articulated columns, there is no question of correct classical references. However, the articulation is too tactile for the pure International Style. There is a clear proportional relationship between the columns and the spanning members between them, and these are plastically enriched in a manner that evokes the classical ideal. The closest resemblance is perhaps to some of the Classic Revival structures of the eighteenth century. Lincoln Center evokes palazzi more than factories.

It seems impossible, however, to find any deep and important distinction between the Lincoln Center complex and the Campidoglio as far as style is concerned. To limit a definition of classicism to a particular family of details is to restrict the relevance of the distinction, and the difference between the classical and the modern becomes insignificant.

It is more sensible to recognize the essential classical content of Lincoln Center and affirm the existence of a contemporary classicism that differs only in detail from the classicism of past ages. This is not to deny the revivalist strain in classicism that continues to assert the intrinsic vitality of the old system of proportion and detail. It is rather to begin to clarify the issue of what is really modern and why it needs to be the way it is. Where Lincoln Center goes wrong is encapsulated in the detailing of the base of the columns at Philharmonic Hall. A slim reveal is meant, one supposes, to express

INTRODUCTION

Figure 7. Campidoglio. Palazzo Nuovo. Elevation of bay.

Figure 8. New York State Theater. Elevation of bay.

Figure 9. Lincoln Center. Philharmonic Hall. Harrison & Abramovitz, 1962. Detail of columns.

the cladding nature of the travertine. But the effect is of the insubstantiality of what should be monumental gravity and weight. There is an essential confusion of classical and modern styles that is symptomatic of a lack of understanding about the nature of each and how they may relate.

Lincoln Center is one in a series of attempts in New York and other cities, particularly in the United States, to transform the nature of a neighborhood through zoning, finance, and the power of eminent domain. Such "renewal" projects were attempted before in the 1920s. Today's Rockefeller Center was originally planned to be a similar renewal project, removing existing low-income housing so that office space could be built. In fact, the office space proved to be potentially so valuable that the Metropolitan Opera—originally to be provided a new home as the focus of the project, as later at Lincoln Center—was finally replaced in that scheme by the skating rink that is still there today. The original building for the Museum of Modern Art was part of this plan, replacing some theaters for African Americans who had been displaced to Harlem by the Pennsylvania Station redevelopment thirty years before.

The empire-building aspects of Lincoln Center are important in understanding the classical elements of the design. Classicism meant tradition, centralized power, and money, even in "modern" garb. It was what was "good for you." The classical composition of Rockefeller Center is thus explained as well, and one may begin to understand the strange blankness of the "modern" skyscrapers along Sixth Avenue that made up the postwar phase of the Center's development. They are "modern" works that express little about the nature of modern life except that it is dense. These buildings are carefully designed and massed to incorporate a classical symmetry and balance, but they have

15

INTRODUCTION

Figure 10. Lincoln Center. Vivian Beaumont Theater. Eero Saarinen, 1965.

nothing to say, no more than the main plaza of Lincoln Center itself.

In decided contrast is the adjacent plaza for the Vivian Beaumont Repertory Theater, designed by Eero Saarinen. Here, the relation between inner and outer, between the space of the plaza and the public space within the lobby, is entirely different. The protecting colonnades of its larger neighbors are absent from the Saarinen building. The overhanging roof slab defines a perimeter, not as a hard-edge screen to be penetrated but as a "zone" of shelter that increases as one penetrates the glazed lobby wall. The relation between the mass of the building and the plaza is therefore negotiable. The structure, although massive, is expressed as light in weight. The plaza reaches into the space in a way that does not even occur at the neighboring Metropolitan Opera House.

Such a relationship is unknown in classical architecture. To set up a dynamic balance whereby a space can be both part of the outside and part of the inside simultaneously is characteristic of modernism.

The Sydney Opera House

An interesting comparison can be made between the cultural center built at Sydney in the 1970s and the near-contemporary Lincoln Center. Published photographs of other entries to the Sydney competition are in stark contrast to Jörn Utzon's famous design. In fact, they resemble Lincoln Center: isolated rectangular blocks facing across a plaza. It is said that Eero Saarinen, architect of the Vivian Beaumont Theater, personally recommended the Utzon scheme which had been initially rejected.

Utzon's buildings are recognized masterpieces of modern architecture. In form and construction technology, they are inconceivable from the point of view of any century but the twentieth. It is pertinent in this regard to acknowledge the profound change in construction techniques that took place during the design development of this project. Initially, the shells were of thin, light-weight design, similar in construction if not configuration to Saarinen's Kresge Auditorium at MIT. But the implementation of this construction turned out to be impossible, and the design was changed to a system of heavy, precast concrete arches built up from modular sections and using advanced techniques in fabrication to avoid the expense of centering. The delicacy of the point supports for the clearly immense masonry masses is a surpassingly modernist vision.

The Sydney Opera House has become as much a symbol of Sydney as the Parthenon on its Acropolis is of Athens. It is important to emphasize that, far from being driven by technological advances, the design of the complex determined the choice of construction methods and materials and even, according to contemporary accounts, required the development of new techniques for its realization.

Why does one cultural complex remind us of a Renaissance masterpiece four hundred years older (and intentionally so according to the architects involved), when its contemporary is purely of the twentieth century? How can both facilities, similar as they are in function, be considered the same in style, that is, modern?

The key to this dilemma lies, in this particular case, in *the intention of the architects*. It has been true since the appearance of an overt, self-conscious Modern Movement that the choice between the classical and modern styles represents an assertion of particular values, an approach to life and how it ought to be lived. The implications of these choices have not changed significantly since before the birth

INTRODUCTION

Figure 11. Restaurant, Sydney Opera House. Jörn Utzon, 1957 ff.

of modernism, and it goes back at least to the founding of the American democracy in the United States and the ideas of Thomas Jefferson.

Methodology

Serious makers of architectural form derive new ideas from what they see around them. In other words, what they create is based on what has come before, even in the case of modern styles. Unlike their predecessors, however, modern architects seek to free themselves from what they perceive as constraints from the past. The study that follows, therefore, is based on a historical examination of key works demonstrating the emergence of modern architecture at the physical, functional, and cultural levels. These works are seen in their sociocultural context through citations from contemporary writings and images.

To this end, the implications of the development of classicism and modernism over the past two hundred years will be examined in a sequence of four phases: historical, technological, cultural, and formal. Chapter 1, which deals with the political and geographical circumstances of this period as well as history, concentrates on three significant trends: the growth of democratic forms of government, the economic development of the American continents, and the archaeological studies of the ancient monuments in Greece and Rome. Chapter 2, on technology, discusses the abstraction of human knowledge, including the impact of industrialization and the effects of enormous growth in science and education. Then Chapter 3 explores the change in scale of civilization, the new self-awareness that has developed, and how it has manifested itself in artistic expression. Finally, Chapter 4 examines the relationship of the historical, technological, and cultural phases to the formal and shows their visible impact on architecture.

Chapter 1

HISTORY: FROM OLIGARCHY TO DEMOCRACY

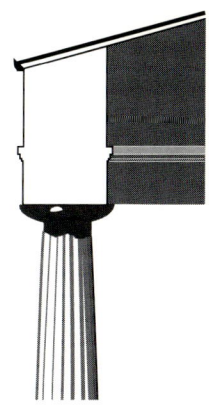

The birth and growth of modernism coincides with the birth and growth of democracy in North and South America, France, and other Western nations. This vast topic, on which libraries of volumes have been written, yields two themes that support the main thrust of the present study: first, a change in focus from the society to the individual and, second, an expansion of common knowledge far beyond the grasp of any individual in his or her lifetime. The focus of eighteenth century society on a model of the cultured gentleman—a member of a privileged class with enough leisure to attain a balanced, general knowledge of the world—changes abruptly by the end of that century to the common man who, through specialized learning of some kind, can mold or shape or direct society in a way that, although beneficial, is unpredictable. A static model of balance is replaced with a dynamic model of progress.

How is this to be seen in the realm of architecture? Through the recognition of a general change in scale: from that which can be controlled through exclusivity to that which applies to all inclusively, resulting in an inevitable loss of control. It is exemplified in the change from the church and palace as the armature of architectural development to the dwelling unit and office building.

The revolutions in France and America were manifestations of a decisive cultural break in Western history, heralded by the widespread distribution of correctly measured drawings of the remains of ancient buildings in Greece and Rome. There is a conceptual gulf between the Late Baroque period and the neoclassicism of the nineteenth century. A new level of abstraction appeared with the scientific application of general rules of design derived from ancient models.

When industrialization and a new understanding of economics focused attention on the creation of wealth, the construction of buildings became professionalized. By historical chance, a new continent was populated by European people at a time when the seeds of revolution were being sown in the homeland. Later, the Civil War in the United States between 1861 and 1865 caused a rupture between the industrializing, mercantile North—whose rejection of its European roots proved to be most profound—and the traditional, agrarian

South whose connections to the class-ridden societies of Europe proved to be much more deeply lodged.

It can be seen that both modernism and the modern version of classicism developed simultaneously in the nineteenth century. They were two distinct and unresolvable bodies of theory. The classicists believe that the shapes and forms developed initially in ancient Greece have proved over time to be the most successful for creating monumentality in architecture and that their meaning has become timeless and universal. The modernists believe that the timeless and universal principles that may be derived from classical design should be applied with contemporary technology and materials, and respond in a progressive way to the modern world.

Modernism itself stems from the European tradition. Its blossoming as a distinct stylistic movement is connected with the codification of classicism at the Ecole des Beaux-Arts. This brought about a self-consciousness that enabled modern designers to both respond to and deny classicism. The mathematics of the generating rules could be readily separated from their application in accordance with neoclassical shapes and details. This intellectualization of culture is a defining determinant of the growth of what we know today as modernism in art and architecture.

As a result of the intellectualization of culture, the idea of space became primary in discussions about the birth of modernism. The classical model of architecture included no such concept. In this model, architecture was the play of solid forms in light. This is not to say that subtle and sophisticated spaces are not elements of classical architecture but rather that classical space is always considered a direct concomitant of an opposition of solid and void in which the solid is dominant.

The notion of space as a positive rather than negative, as the generator of a building, is crucial to understanding modernism. Certainly, previous eras have questioned the primacy of solid building forms. The High Gothic cathedrals, with their dissolution of solids into light-filled glass cages, is an obvious example. Another is the Late Baroque era, in which the spatial action began to distort the structure of buildings. A more subtle example is the Gothic style in England in the fourteenth and fifteenth centuries when fan vaulting brought a deeper questioning of the nature of architectural substance. But none of these historical trends succeeded in achieving the idea of an *independent space,* a volume defined by function and purpose whose interaction with a containing structure is not entirely predictable.

Inseparable from the development of modern architecture is the growth of the industrial and commercial city, perceived as a great change in the scale of buildings. New York is the best source for studying the development of the modern vision, the concentration of tall buildings at its core having occurred before the advent of distinctively modern styles. Chicago is problematic from this point of view, since its great fire of 1871 had cleared much of the downtown area, freeing up large building sites. Also difficult to study are the cities of Europe, since they remained low-rise in nature until the extensive rebuilding following World War II. It must be remembered, in this context, that the social goals of CIAM (Congrès Internationaux d'architecture moderne), the primary exponent of the International Style in the 1930s and 1940s, was first the provision of much-needed low-cost housing and later the rebuilding or replacement of devastated urban facilities. This gave a pragmatic aspect to what has been called the "Utopian" thrust of modernism, though in America nothing could be more Utopian than "The City Beautiful", a neoclassic vision that drove much of city planning from the 1893 Columbian Exposition in Chicago through World War I. Daniel Burnham and

McKim, Mead & White are among the leading American architects who promoted this vision. For example, many of the major railroad stations in the United States were built according to its principles.

It is important for any careful study of modern architecture to distinguish social and economic forces that may be determining the form of buildings from the esthetic choices available to designers. Many modern buildings have been criticized for their size and lack of fine detailing, and justly so, but there is often little control over such factors by the architects involved. Modern buildings are larger and cheaper than older buildings and much of the success of the International Style was its adaptability to large-scale development. When the great change in scale in building occurred around the turn of the twentieth century, office buildings and mass housing projects came to represent substantially new ways of comprehending cities. Nevertheless, it is certainly true that modern architectural theory has attempted to address these trends, and this study will aim for a balanced evaluation of the results.

SPACE

An image of solids in light is the basis for the classical idea of space. The opposition of solid and void is treated as a unity in the architectural continuum. Solids always have mass; space is always that-which-is-not-solid. Because of this, classical architecture is in a sense an art of edges. The importance of the corners, sharp lines, and subtle curves of classical elements was greatly enhanced during the neoclassical period, when a white or monochromatic architecture, devoid for the most part of color or surface pattern, was preferred, in spite of historical investigations at Pompeii and Herculaneum which revealed the ancient taste for exuberant decoration.

In the nineteenth century, the dissemination of information about classical buildings increased by orders of magnitude with each new development in printing and publishing. Almost all of the graphics consisted of line drawings reproduced through some form of engraving or lithography. This greatly increased the tendency to see classical architecture in a linear manner, as monochromatic solids rendered three-dimensional by edges and shadows. The abstraction of mathematical rules for generating correct proportions supported this trend.

To modern designers, space is a field of action, either real or potential. The same techniques of publishing that presented classical forms in a linear way also could make visible the lines that generated the plans and sections. The professionalization of architectural practice included the standardization of drawing for construction. Architectural drawing gradually increased the abstraction of architectural design to a point where a space could be rendered as easily as a structure.

This concept of increasing abstraction was remarked upon in 1849 by John Ruskin, the chief proponent of the Gothic Revival and a notorious anticlassicist:

> the two conditions of [the art of design] which are essentially architectural [are],—Proportion and Abstraction. Neither of these qualities is necessary, to the same extent, in other fields of design. . . . Architecture . . . delights in Abstraction and fears to complete her forms.   [1]

The source of this abstraction is in the professional practice of design itself. The architect does not build a building, but draws and writes a set of instructions on how the building is to be constructed. The tools of the trade are not hammer and saw, but pen and straightedge. When the two-dimensional drawings are interpreted in the world of three-dimensional materiality, planes become surfaces or slabs, and lines

become edges or joints. The classical architect will seek to coordinate this process so that the drawing and building form a complete package.

In classical design, the technology of drawing—and even of developing a design—is irrelevant. It is the final product, solid forms rendered in light, that is all-important, and it should appear inevitable and timeless. The Beaux-Arts techniques of realistic rendering were perfectly suited to classical designs. The modern architect will emphasize the distinction between design phases, recording the process of design in the material building. There is a sense in which a modern building is a composite of planar elements and extrusions, explicating itself as the viewer passes through it. It is a quality of architecture that corresponds to the Cubist vision in painting.

Enclosure

One of the tenets of Beaux-Arts planning is said to be the clear separation of function by architectural elements. But at a deeper level, this means the separation of social classes, for classical propriety dictated who got to perform which function. This attitude can be discerned in a quotation from Edith Wharton's *The Decoration of Houses:*

> Privacy would seem to be one of the first requisites of civilized life, yet it is only necessary to observe the planning and arrangement of the average house to see how little this need is recognized . . . whatever the uses of a room, they are seriously interfered with if it be not preserved as a small world by itself. . . . It may be that architect and decorator live in a simpler manner than their clients, and are therefore ready to sacrifice a kind of comfort of which they do not feel the need to the "effects" obtainable by vast openings and extended "vistas." 2

Wharton's book is an important milestone in the development of classicism, appearing in 1902 just six years before Frank Lloyd Wright's articles began appearing in the *Architectural Record*. Her work is a record of the social meaning of classical forms that survives even today.

Classical buildings were designed for ceremonial activities that emphasized the distinction of social position. Sequences of space were used to define one's closeness to the source of power. A notable example is the landscaping in vogue during the eighteenth century in France, where the sequence of *parterre, bosquet,* and *selvatico* indicated increasing distance from *le roi* and, therefore, from civilization itself.

The clear distinction of primary and subsidiary spaces is the definitive intention behind classical architecture. It is, for example, the basis of Palladio's style. He distinguishes the important from the less important through symmetrical placement and centrality, as well as through the size and richness of surface detail.

The compartmentalization of function that is characteristic of the Beaux-Arts would seem to be appropriate for the functionalist approach of modern architecture. But modern architects are interested in relating functions, themselves well defined, rather than separating them. In modern designs, for example, circulation through a room is seen as a coordination of movement and stasis that can in combination generate a unique space. The ideal classical solution, in contrast, would be to provide a separate circulation element, such as a corridor, to distinguish the two uses.

Exclusive versus Inclusive

The organization of a classical system requires that it be closed. Whatever cannot be worked into the hierarchy is excluded from the design and indeed from any identity as an architectural object. Modernism, in contrast, is essentially open and even includes that which is not definable. A work of modern design is always incomplete in a certain sense.

The question of the classical versus the modern has come to mean, in architecture unlike any of the other arts, the value of tradition measured against the value of the new. It is a deeply serious question for the contemporary world, in which technical knowledge enables some societies to expand economically far more than—and perhaps at the expense of—others. Architecture reveals this discrepancy directly, as one recognizes immediately upon considering Brasilia, the International Style capital of Brazil sitting in the middle of an Amazon jungle, or Le Corbusier's capitol complex at Chandigarh, surrounded by the hovels of the dispossessed.

So when one questions the nature of modernism, it is more than an argument about style, or even esthetics. When Penn Station in New York City, an acknowledged Beaux-Arts masterpiece, was demolished to make way for an indifferently designed office and sports complex in the International Style—thereby spawning the local preservation movement—issues of social and civic value were raised. When the Guggenheim Museum sells some of its Kandinskis to obtain resources for acquisition, one may regret the loss, but there is no question of destroying the paintings. Again, it is difficult for modern composers that civic orchestras must schedule a classical piece to guarantee public attendance at a concert, but no one proposes burning anyone's scores. However, for a modern building to be put up, very often an older building must first be removed, and one is dealing much more deeply with social values. Even if nothing is to be destroyed, a very fine modern building may yet harm a neighborhood of consistent classical style, where the individual buildings themselves may be of indifferent quality. It must be stated, however, that part of the intention of modern architecture is to address its environment and include all of the existing qualities that characterize it. Aldo Rossi develops this idea at length in *The Architecture of the City*.

> [Architecture is] inseparable from civilized life and the society in which it is manifested. By nature it is collective. As the first men built houses to provide more favorable surroundings for their life, fashioning an artificial climate for themselves, so they built with aesthetic intention. Architecture came into being along with the first traces of the city; it is deeply rooted in the formation of civilization and is a permanent, universal, and necessary artifact.
>
> Aesthetic intention and the creation of better surroundings for life are the two permanent characteristics of architecture. These aspects emerge from any significant attempt to explain the city as a human creation. But because architecture gives concrete form to society and is intimately connected with it and with nature, it differs fundamentally from every other art and science. . . . The contrast between particular and universal, between individual and collective, emerges from the city and from its construction, its architecture.   3

Here, of course, one begins to distinguish modernism itself, for the truly modern is always *inclusive*; whether it comments upon the classical, denies it, mocks it, or attempts to respond to it, a serious modern work embodies the principles of classicism as an aspect of the whole. Correct classicism itself, however, whether of 1490 or 1990, seeks to differentiate itself from its environment. It is self-contained and *exclusive* in nature.

The Relation to Nature
One of the most profound changes that have come about in Western societies is in humankind's relationship with the

natural world. The exclusionary quality of classical architecture was enhanced, in northern climates, by a desire for protection against nature rather than continuity with nature. In this sense alone, some of the ancient sensibility about architecture must have been lost, since the Greeks and Romans inhabited temperate climates. The enclosure of formal gardens in northern Europe in the seventeenth and eighteenth centuries and the geometric nature of their layouts demonstrated a new attitude of control over the environment by man.

The transformation of humankind's relation to the natural world for modern architecture can be described in two stages. The first, coincident with the industrial revolution, is a sense of power over natural things that enables their utilization for economic gain. The effect on the American landscape of the building of railroads during the nineteenth and early twentieth centuries has been enormous, not only in direct physical changes but also in the homogenization of culture resulting from quick and easy transit between distant places. The second stage of the transformation has appeared in the late twentieth century and is characterized by a protective, caretaking outlook for the natural world which seeks once again to build in a manner more in accord with natural forces. The latter idea requires a faith in one's understanding of nature, an idea that it is neither mysterious nor dangerous, and it represents a complete transformation of humankind's sensitivity to the environment.

The transparency of modern buildings allows a new kind of connection with nature that supports the modern view. It is in accord with the control over interior climate that has been made possible by advanced mechanical systems. The modern interior is abstract, universal, and completely adjustable to the comfort of occupants, regardless of outside conditions. This is what Le Corbusier meant when he called the modern dwelling *une machine d'habiter*.

Private and Public Places

The nature of work underwent a transformation between the eighteenth century and the twentieth. Industrialization called for new skills in manual labor, and the enormous growth of paperwork meant changes in the way labor was performed and how it was valued. Democratic societies have placed a higher value on work than on leisure, partly because work has become more a thing of the mind. During the Enlightenment of the eighteenth century, mental activity was a luxury available to few. In the modern world, mental activity has been professionalized.

Consequently, the workplace has become an important building type. Classical architecture did not define prototypical places for work, because such models generally did not exist. There certainly were factories and shops, but these accommodated the trade rather than the function and were rarely considered worthy of attention from architects.

In the modern world, however, work has become a public function. The organization of commerce in the industrial city has established social stratifications based on the sort of work one does rather than one's family lineage. Work is for most people a major social interaction.

The greatest example of the change is of course the commercial skyscraper. Its articulation of windowed bays emphasizes the new scale of enterprise. The three-dimensional grid is an important spatial archetype for the modern world. Miës van der Rohe perfected this type in his Cartesian skyscrapers, which express the infinite extensibility of modern space, even and unchanging in all three directions. When this extensibility is contrasted to the material limitations of structure, engineering, and economics, a modern continuum is expressed. Miës's tendency, however, was toward harmony of these elements and he was more of a classicist than he is usually assumed to be.

Outside and Inside

Classical planning seeks to control the degree of enclosure through establishing an organized system of walls, arcades, and colonnades that control one's perception of space. This is a natural concomitant of the fixed duality between solid and void expressed by classical architecture. The experience of a classical building includes a hierarchy of spaces determined by ceiling height, degree of articulation, and finishes.

The development of new construction materials in the nineteenth century undermined the strict hierarchy. Steel and reinforced concrete supporting structures were flexible enough to replace bearing walls, which meant that the extension of the roof overhead need not follow the location of walls. The plans of Frank Lloyd Wright's early Prairie houses show this relationship directly. When flexibility of structure is combined with the availability of large sheets of glass, the whole question of inside and outside becomes moot.

This is most strikingly evident in one of the archetypal precursors to modernism, the Crystal Palace pavilion of 1858. Enclosed entirely with iron-framed glass for a temporary exhibition, it stood in a park and was transparent, from both inside and outside. In spite of its immense size, the Crystal Palace reduced its presence to no more than that of an enormous umbrella, a minimal enclosure. Regardless of social position, anyone was free to enter and wander at will among the exhibits.

Historically, the Crystal Palace's greatest significance may finally lie in its complete accessibility to the public. In the modern world, access to great spaces is no longer a sign of social status. The great railroad stations built in major American cities in the early twentieth century resulted from huge public works projects driven solely by questions of traffic circulation—rail, road, and foot. They were typically split into two parts: a classically configured waiting room and ticket office adjoining a large, glassed-roof area over the train platforms. The corridor, that ultimate Beaux-Arts symbol of controlled procession, is replaced by the concourse.

Climate

One of the great influences on the history of Western architecture is the change in focus of design from southern Europe to northern Europe, first in the Middle Ages and later in the eighteenth century. Much of the richness of the classical vocabulary derives from the adjustments necessary between environments that may or may not be benevolent.

It can be argued that the medieval Gothic style was really an extension of Imperial Roman classicism adapted for darkness, rain, and cold. By the eighteenth century, however, the classical style had adapted itself well to the climates of England, Russia, and the Scandinavian countries, not to mention the new colonies in America.

This trend of abstraction from the environment continued with the development of modern styles. Machinery to control indoor temperatures has become so sophisticated that exterior conditions are all but irrelevant to modern life. The function that takes place within buildings goes on year-round, and International Style skyscrapers are truly international in scope.

Social Interaction

During the great ages of classicism, proximity to royalty was a major determinant of social status. Indeed, the planning of

the royal palace at Versailles focused on the bed of the king. To be *inside* the king's circle was to avoid being *outside* the social circle. The hierarchy of functions that classical architecture was developed to define depended on a strict system of social class. The dissolution of a rigidly determined class system led to the more open society of the modern world, characterized in contrast by social mobility.

Modern architecture has sought to provide for just such dynamic relationships. The blandness that is often perceived is a direct result of functional universality. As modernism developed through the twentieth century, an identification with classicism has come to mean an identification with tradition. Classical architecture is upscale and expensive. Its legitimate visual appeal suggests order and harmony in a world perceived as difficult and dissonant.

Solid and Void

One of the great esthetic changes that drove the development of modern architecture was the concept of independent space. Looking at photographs of the Crystal Palace through modern eyes, one can see the volume of the enclosed space as easily as the light structure that defined it. It is very significant that John Ruskin's *The Seven Lamps of Architecture* does not mention space or volume, let alone talk about spatial concepts. Ninety years later, Siegfried Giedion defined the history of architecture in terms of space:

> There are three stages of architectural development. During the first stage—the first space conception—space was brought into being by the interplay between volumes. This stage encompassed the architecture of Egypt, Sumer, and Greece. Interior space was disregarded.
>
> The second space conception began in the midst of the Roman period when interior space and with it the vaulting problem started to become the highest aim of architecture. The Roman Pantheon with its forerunners marks its beginning. During the second space conception, the formation of interior space became synonymous with hollowed-out interior space. Alois Riegl was the first to recognize this. Despite several profound differentiations, this second space conception persisted throughout the period from the Roman Pantheon to the end of the eighteenth century.
>
> The nineteenth century forms an intermediary link. A spatial analysis of its buildings indicates that elements of all the different phases of the second stage are simultaneously intermingled (Paul Frankl). But the earlier spatial unity vanished more and more. Buildings which most truly represented the period were ignored by the public.
>
> The third space conception set in at the beginning of this century with the optical revolution that abolished the single viewpoint of perspective. This had fundamental consequences for man's conception of architecture and the urban scene. The space-emanating qualities of free-standing buildings could again be appreciated. We recognize an affinity with the first space conception. Just as at its beginning, architecture is again approaching sculpture and sculpture is approaching architecture. At the same time the supreme preoccupation of the second space conception—the hollowing out of interior space—is continued, though there is a profoundly different approach to the vaulting problem. New elements have been introduced: a hitherto unknown interpenetration of inner and outer space and an interpenetration of different levels (largely an effect of the automobile), which has forced the incorporation of movement as an inseparable element of architecture. All these have contributed to the space conception of the present day and underlie its evolving tradition. 4

This statement marks a significant historical change. In reinterpreting history, it incorporates an entirely new understanding of human action, of the place of humanity in the universe. It raises human thought to a new level of abstraction.

Profoundly an idea of the perception of the individual, the idea of space has no collective meaning and cannot be impressed into the service of supporting a social hierarchy. To interpret the classical tradition in terms of space is to devalue it as a social force, whatever understanding may be gained

The Meaning of Walls

As Palladio so elegantly demonstrated, the articulation of the wall is elemental to classical design. Walls represent substance, solidity, and material. Their essential quality is weight. The goal of articulation is to express that weight in a coherent manner. For this reason, columns must sit upon bases or pedestals, ranges must rest on arcades, and these in turn must rest on solid walls. The thickness of solid walls must be reinforced by moldings and frames. The detailing of all of the parts must represent the whole for perfect coherence.

The perfection of classical detailing depends on the surface of masses rendered in light and shadow. Abstraction in classicism depends on the essential materiality of masonry. Although thin sheets of finished stone were typically used over rough brick, these were detailed to appear solid. This abstraction of the surface permitted freedom in decoration. The material manifestation of this abstraction was enhanced by the idea of purity when Athenian buildings were measured and described in the late eighteenth century.

The transparency and lightness of modern buildings eludes classical criticism. Modern skyscrapers are much larger than classical buildings but are detailed to express lightness rather than mass. Glass as it is used in modern buildings has a dynamic quality that appears either solid or transparent depending on lighting conditions. Where mass is expressed, as in Eero Saarinen's CBS building in New York, it is contrasted to the lightness of the interior space. This International Style skyscraper is supported by its exterior walls in a manner similar to classical structures rather than the more typical steel cage. Yet the perception of interior space is perfectly clear. The exterior can be seen as both mass and cage, a simultaneous reading characteristic of modern architecture.

Support

The classical structural system is based on masonry walls held together by weight and internal pressure. Lighter elements sit upon weighty elements and the whole must be detailed to reflect visually coherent support. This usually means a vertical sequence of floors from a rusticated base through a series of colonnaded stories to a cornice.

Modern buildings express a separation between support and space. In the CBS building, the supporting columns are aggregated as a wall of dense masonry. Their spacing is such that they can be seen individually, as triangular columns, or *en masse* as a wall, undifferentiated as it rises and terminated simply, without cap or cornice of any kind.

GEOMETRY

Along with the general growth of the sciences, geometry expanded into a discrete field of knowledge that included close ties with pure logic and philosophy. Indeed, the teaching of mathematics even at the level of public high schools included basic geometry as the best means to demonstrate the logical proofs of algebra. The tie between geometry and logic is important, for the Enlightenment sought to derive all knowledge from some method of logical proof. The famous Modulor system of measurement and proportion developed by Le Corbusier in the 1940s demonstrates how closely remain the ties between geometry and pure reason.

The development of modern architecture thus retained this closeness, along with the elements of classical geometry: the use of a repetitive grid, reduction of parts to simple geometric shapes, and so forth. The main difference was in modern architecture's interest in the intersection, or collision, of independent systems. More than one geometrical system

HISTORY:
FROM
OLIGARCHY
TO
DEMOCRACY

Figure 12. CBS Building, New York. Eero Saarinen, 1965.

would be at work in a modern building, in direct contrast to classical principles.

Cartesian Solids

The geometry of classical architecture, as it was taught in the nineteenth century, was based on the Cartesian solids and their planar projections. The cube and the square, the sphere and the circle, the pyramid and the equilateral triangle: these were the main sources of shapes for architectural elements. Because they are restrictive and difficult to use, variations were permitted, especially in the case of rectangles, by far the most useful geometric shape for buildings.

Other basic curves became part of the vocabulary of geometry through the description of algebraic equations. These curves, of which the circle is a special case, are called the *conic sections*, because they are derived from the intersection in three dimensions of a cone and a plane. It might seem likely that these curves—the parabola, hyperbola, and ellipse—would form the basis of modern architecture, but that is not so. They have certainly been used, particularly for structural challenges such as thin-shell roofs and bridge supports, but sophisticated engineering developed other forms in the nineteenth century, such as the catenary curve, which is familiar in suspension bridges. Modern design has tended instead toward the collision of classical solids and lines in unpredictable ways. This does not mean chaos in design: it means the incorporation of unpredictability into the design of systems.

Meaning in Order

A classically designed building is an assembly of related parts designed to form a cohesive whole. The pyramid of the main roof would be echoed by a smaller pediment over the central portico and individual pediments over the main windows and doors. All of these pediments would, according to Beaux-Arts principles, have similar angles. The richness of the classical model is in its accommodation of disparate parts into a coherent system. The Cartesian shapes are the basis for all design.

A modern building will also include the systematization of parts, but with two important distinctions: the parts may be expressed as an indeterminate repetition of elements so that they generate the system, reversing the classical hierarchy. The other main difference is that completely different systems, mutually incoherent, will be used together in a way that reveals their collision.

Size and Scale

The change in the use of geometric principles in the modern era reflects a change in the scope of human knowledge. The growth of democracy focused attention on the individual rather than on the whole. In America especially, this necessitated the inclusion of a great many different cultures, all of which had been based on foreign models. The Native American cultures were all but extinguished. The result was a sort of inevitable blandness, or generic modern culture, that was spread around the world in the twentieth century. This is not to say that great variety was not possible. To the contrary, the cities of Boston, New Orleans, and Los Angeles are more distinct than those of many other countries because of the difference in their ethnic backgrounds. Nevertheless, the modernization of these and other cities has tended to reduce the differences, establishing a vocabulary of building, street, and highway that seems to be the Esperanto of design.

During the nineteenth century, the growth of scientific knowledge expanded far beyond any one individual's capacity to understand it. Thus the disappearance of the classical gentleman (for women were not often educated in science), whose essential character was generalized knowledge. One of the last was Thomas Jefferson.

The change in the size and scale of culture was reflected in a change of focus in architecture from the monumental palace and church to the private house and the office building. One was too small and the other too large for a completely successful application of Beaux-Arts principles. However, an otherwise plain row of abutting houses could be given charming classical porticos and details, uniting them into a pleasing composition. London owes much of its appeal to this design approach. Nonetheless it remains true that the most convincing classical buildings are the size of a palace.

Plasticity

The growth of science also brought about the development of modern building materials and rational details to follow in construction. Much of the craft of building was transferred to the architect and engineer, who assumed responsibility for the performance of buildings by controlling how they were made. The intellectualization of this process changed completely the classical understanding of elemental substance. Now, a series of layers of dissimilar components made up the construction of walls. And the walls themselves became free of supporting structures, designed independently and incorporated into the construction scheme through careful and extensive detailing of connections between the parts. The technical requirements of walls increased as their role in controlling climate and view was enhanced.

The result was a change in the nature of plasticity, from the sculptural, tactile expression of classical art and architecture to a light, planar flatness that appeared not only in architecture but in early modern painting as well. From the Impressionists to the Cubists, traditional rendering of

solids in light was ignored in favor of examinations of light, surfaces, and spaces themselves.

The classical wall was conceived of as essential stuff, undifferentiated *poché,* as shown in sections drawn at the time. The surface was meant to be finished according to its exposure. Exterior walls were to be of in rough or dressed stone. Interior walls might be lined with wood, fabric, or plaster that itself might be painted or frescoed.

In modern architecture, the substance of the wall has its own quality. Its material is specific and has significance for the design. The Brutalist style of the 1950s and 1960s emphasized the expression of raw concrete and rusting steel as finishes. As dictated by contemporary theory, flat, unarticulated surfaces rendered white are universal, pure, and "background," perfect for the display of fine art. All the evidence accumulated by the Gestalt psychologists and others points to the impossibility of "turning off" one's perception of substance, solidity, and surface. Nevertheless, the myth of the white space continues with little of the resistance from modern designers that the neoclassical movement met in its own time. Both modern and classical manifestations have more to do with the attempt to construct images of line drawings than with any real understanding of the perception of material.

The Importance of Craft

As the industrial revolution transformed the craft of building, readily available paper and printing technologies transformed the dissemination of building knowledge. Learning about construction changed from a craft learned on the job through an apprentice system to a mathematically defined process that included drawing and writing of specifications and contracts. Architecture, and to a great extent building itself, became abstracted to the point where most architects today play a relatively minor role in the actual construction process. The drawings and other documents that architects prepare are supposed to define completely the structure to be built.

The loss in tactile quality that has occurred is paralleled by the influence of graphics on painting. The scale of paintings was once carefully related to the scale of rooms, reflected in classically correct architectural elements. Today, art is not necessarily scaled to individual perception and is typically huge in comparison to classical work, as are, for example, the Marc Chagall paintings in the Metropolitan Opera House at Lincoln Center. The resulting dissociation between the individual and the work of art parallels the lack of intimacy so often criticized in modern architecture.

Realism

The subject of architecture underwent a profound change in the modern era. Classical buildings attempt to elucidate a social hierarchy through the relation of design elements. Important spaces housing major functions must be differentiated and separated from lesser elements. Interior decoration was geared to the maintaining of privacy and social distinction.

> There are two ways of being in scale: there is the scale of proportion, and what might be called the scale of appropriateness. The former is a matter of actual measurement, while the latter is regulated solely by the nicer standard of good taste. 5

The modern era is frequently known as the machine age, and certainly the phenomenon of mass production has been an important concern of modernism. But late in the nineteenth century there also occurred a trend toward functionalism, quite different from mechanization. This included the close examination of human function and paralleled the revolutionary incorporation of plumbing and electrical services into ordinary houses. Zoning and building codes also became prevalent, defining the size and scale of building units according to minimum standards, which, in the nature of such things, are more usually considered the norm than the minimum.

The focus began to change in the nineteenth century to include the ordinary as well as the great. Emerson saw it thus:

> I read with joy some of the auspicious signs of the coming days as they glimmer already through poetry and art, through philosophy and science, through church and state.
>
> One of these signs is the fact that the same movement which effected the elevation of what was called the lowest class in the state, assumed in literature a very marked and as benign an aspect. Instead of the sublime and beautiful, the near, the low, the common, was explored and poetized. That which had been negligently trodden under foot by those who were harnessing and provisioning themselves for long journeys into far countries, is suddenly found to be richer than all foreign parts. The literature of the poor, the feelings of the child, the philosophy of the street, the meaning of household life, are the topics of the time. It is a great stride. It is a sign—is it not? of new vigor, when the extremities are made active, when currents of warm life run into the hands and the feet. I ask not for the great, the remote, the romantic; what is doing in Italy or Arabia; what is Greek art, or Provencal Minstrelsy; I embrace the common, I explore and sit at the feet of the familiar, the low. Give me insight into to-day, and you may have the antique and future worlds. . . . the world lies no longer a dull miscellany and lumber room, but has form and order; there is no trifle; there is no puzzle; but one design unites and animates the farthest pinnacle and the lowest trench. 6

The subject of architecture, then, can be said to have changed from the structure of a civilized society to the development of the individual within a society. Classical architecture is representational in that it refers to the buildings of earlier times. The adaptation of older models is one of the important techniques of classical design. That this technique has been problematic for modern architecture is exemplified at Lincoln Center.

Coordination of Systems

To the degree that the components of a building are indeed organized into visually coherent systems, the building can be said to be a work of architecture. It requires more than the mere construction of a habitable shell, no matter how well it may be crafted. It also requires more than the application of some pictorial "effect" or "image." Architecture engages the visual sense in a coherent manner. It is never chaotic, although it may represent chaos as a subject.

The definitive difference between a classical building and a modern one is how the systems that compose it are organized. Based on a hierarchy of systems and elements, classicism is the richest of the traditional Western types of building because of the flexibility of its parts and the cogency of its rules. The parts are derived from the orders of ancient Greece and Italy: the Tuscan, Doric, Ionic, Corinthian, and Composite models for supporting elements of buildings. These orders define the elements of a strictly detailed and proportioned columnar structure. The parts can be modified and adapted to a wide range of building needs, from square piers to domes and arches.

At the time of the American and French Revolutions at the end of the eighteenth century, a series of archaeological discoveries in Greece and Italy were being published and

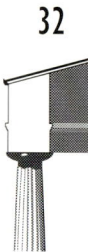

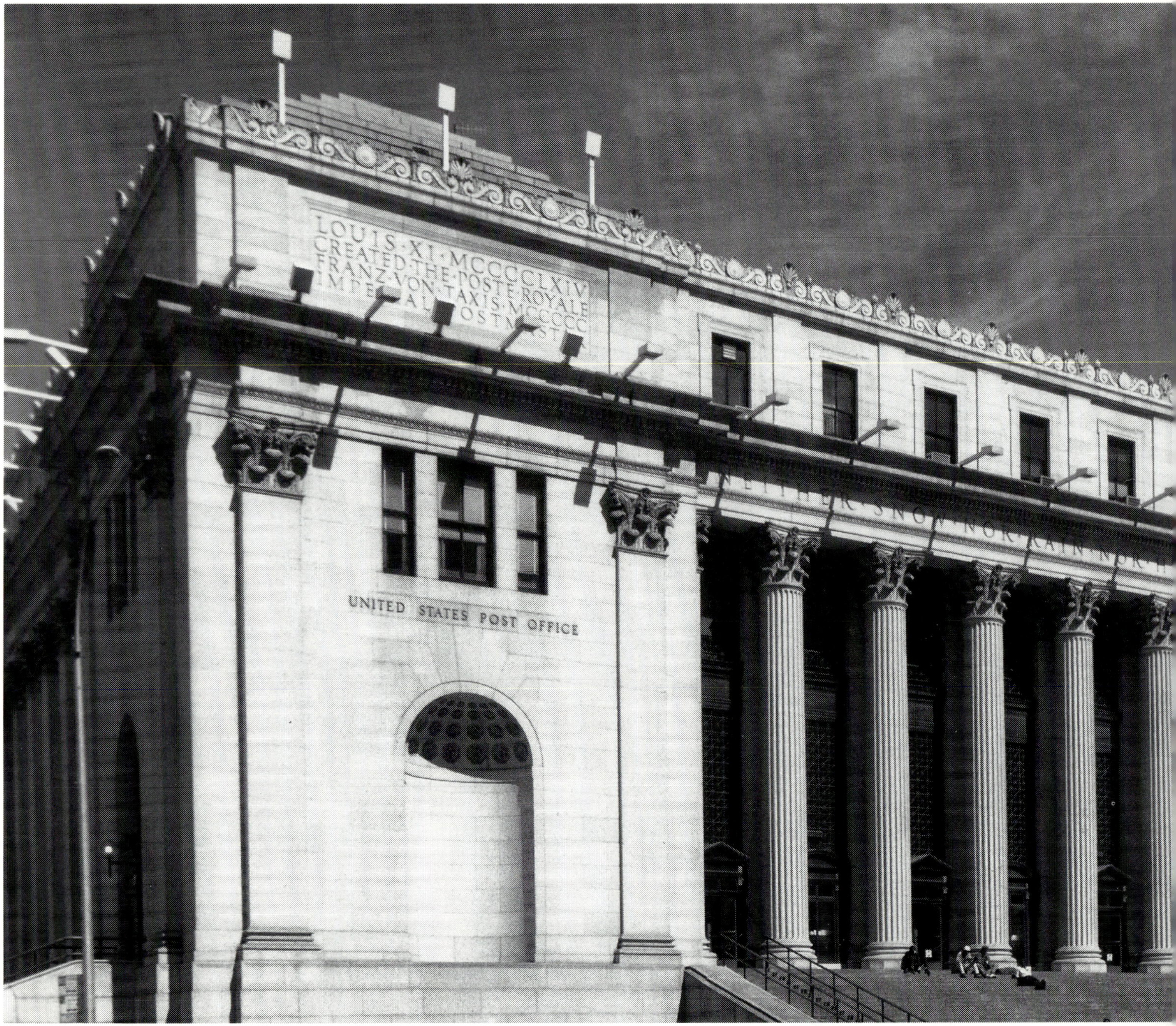
LOUIS·XI·MCCCCLXIV
CREATED·THE·POSTE·ROYALE
FRANZ·VON·TAXIS·MCCCCC
UNITED STATES POST OFFICE

Figure 13. James J. Farley Post Office, New York. McKim, Mead & White, 1912.

33

HISTORY:
FROM
OLIGARCHY
TO
DEMOCRACY

widely circulated among architects. These findings were disseminated in the form of engravings of measured drawings prepared by the discoverers. At the same time, classical Greek sculptures and pieces of ancient temples were brought back to museums and private collections in western Europe, most notably by Lord Elgin in 1806 to the British Museum in London. The result of this new knowledge was a codification of the elements of classical buildings. Called Neoclassical, Greek Revival, and various other names, new architectural movements changed classicism from Late Baroque sophistication to a much simpler and more sober correctness.

At the same time, Gothic Revival buildings had developed, based on antiquarian attention to existing medieval buildings. Although codification of this style was attempted, the more lasting result was a greater understanding of structural engineering and masonry construction. It was the abstraction of principle which generated both revivals that would ultimately spawn the modernism of the twentieth century. Esthetic principles, structural principles, principles of function: all were codified into systems that had no innate relationship to each other. Thus modern architecture, attempting to include them all, would have to find the means of expressing independent ideas simultaneously.

Organization

Classical architecture depends on a strictly defined hierarchy of building systems. Since ancient times, for example, it was considered proper that a Corinthian order could stand upon an Ionic order, which in turn could be supported by a Doric order, but the reverse was incorrect. Major additions to the classical vocabulary were added by Michelangelo with his definition of the giant order in Rome in the early sixteenth century, and by the architect Palladio with his publication of engravings of drawings based on his measurements of ancient Roman buildings and his statement of principles based thereon.

Everything about a classical building supports the subservience of parts to the whole. The principles of centrality, symmetry, and proportion all serve to emphasize a coherent, controlled system and thus it is classical architecture that has most often been the choice of those who wish to exert control over others, from Pope Sixtus V to Josef Stalin.

> When you have a brand-new moneyed class, as you do with the new social class based on tremendous fortunes made in the past ten years on Wall Street and in real estate, they, like Napoleon, are immediately going to make their appeal to authority in the form of classical design.... Neoclassicism will always instate itself when you have a usurping regime or a regime that feels itself to be somewhat upstart: it will base its appeal to authority on the pomposity of Roman design—of Roman interpretations of Greek design. Not even seeing that the Greek is the great classic design, they turn to the ponderous Roman version, with its imperial eagles. Which is, of course, what happened in the United States during the Federal period and the beginnings of this country, when you had a new government in a new country, which was somewhat illegitimate in the eyes of Europe. 7

Modern architecture does not oppose classical principles so much as incorporate them into a larger framework. The key difference is between the classical *hierarchy* of systems and the *equivalence* of modern systems. One of the great planning ideas of classical architecture is the location of an architectural element such as a triumphal arch or obelisk at the intersection of avenues to focus the eye and control a view. Structures such as the Arc de Triomphe of 1806 on the Champs Elysées in Paris, the Washington Monument of

1884 in Washington, D.C., and the Eiffel Tower constructed for the Paris Exhibition of 1889 demonstrate the idea. At the New York World's Fair of 1939, the planning also included avenues whose focus would be a symbol constructed for this purpose. But the symbol consisted of not one but two equivalent forms: the Trylon (a sort of obelisk) and Perisphere (a sphere) whose relationship was not determinable. Together, they formed a symbol that is still recognizable of the modern view of the world before World War II, unlike their more classically disposed replacement, the Unisphere of the 1964 fair, still in place if little remembered.

Mechanization

The rich detailing and careful proportion of classical architecture required handwork by experienced artisans. When the mechanization of building replaced this handwork with reproduced copies fabricated *en masse*, much of the importance of detailing was lost. Although many people today admire and enjoy the beauty of classical work, the meaning of the symbolic details is alien to all but connoisseurs. Ironically, such a situation only supports the social stratification typical of classicism.

What ultimately replaced correct historical ornamentation was the articulation of structural details so typical of modern architecture. A good classical work let you know who you were and how you fit into the scheme of things. Such communication is not available in modernism: you are told instead where to go and how the building was made. Although the classical system was hierarchical, its communication was more intimate than the abstraction of modern detailing. The tactile quality of fine classical design is not generally found in modern architecture; the detailing of the buildings at Lincoln Center is a good example of this.

The Main Post Offices in New York and Chicago

This exploration may be extended to twentieth century masterpieces by two architects in the United States: the James J. Farley Post Office of 1912 in New York by McKim, Mead & White, and the Main Post Office in Chicago of 1968 by Ludwig Miës van der Rohe, who is generally acknowledged as one of the masters of modern architecture. Again, the functional aspects of the two buildings are identical. They were built for the same purpose by the same client and reflect only incidental changes in the sorting and delivery of mail over the fifty years between the completion of the buildings. These changes have little to do with the public areas of either which, in fact, may be seen in both cases to have been far more influenced by the adjoining civic centers than by the selling of stamps. In New York, the post office was designed as part of the Penn Station complex, a manifestation of City Beautiful principles in Manhattan by the same firm who laid out the Mall in Washington, D.C. Its exceedingly correct Corinthian colonnade above a monumental flight of steps faced the Doric colonnade at grade of the railroad station across Eighth Avenue.

Miës's colonnade is of steel-and-glass members, located at grade like Penn Station. Their detailing is as precise and calculated for metal construction as the Farley's is for stone. Both buildings are steel-framed and are similar in proportion. The Farley building is a prime example of the Beaux-Arts classicism of McKim, Mead & White. The Chicago post office is similarly definitive of the style of Miës van der Rohe, a leader of the International Style.

The great difference in appearance between these two examples must depend on the choice of materials and finish. Two elements, then, stand out as defining characteristics. First, the classical building refers to materials, detailing, and propor-

Figure 14. Main Post Office, Chicago. Ludwig Miës van der Rohe, 1968.

tions from a distant past. It asserts the value of tradition through the monumentality of the giant colonnade above its broad stair. All of the trappings of classical grandeur—niches, inscriptions, reliefs—have been beautifully arranged for effect.

The reference to the past, it must be pointed out, is made in spite of the actual conditions of the site. This seemingly weighty stone block is in fact suspended above a network of railroad tracks. It was part of one of the greatest civil engineering projects ever completed: the Manhattan extension of the Pennsylvania Railroad. The purpose of the building was to enable immediate delivery of postal bags to the platform below, adjacent to the departing train. In its time, this represented a great advance in the technology of communication. The fact that its appearance refers to something else entirely suggests that the building is representational in the sense of a neoclassical painting. It has a subject that is not architecture *per se*.

The Chicago post office, on the other hand, refers to abstract principles of minimalist design. Some of these principles—the regularity, the clarity of structure, the attention to use—are shared by the Farley building, since they are the same for classical as for modern design. However, Miës's building does not refer overtly to the distant past, and can be said to be nonreferential in the manner of abstract art.

But there is another difference, more significant for modernism. It is a result of the transparency of the Miës building. The plaza seems to flow continuously through the glass wall of the post office. The interior space in this sense overlaps that of the plaza. When one occupies the post office, one hasn't left the plaza. In contrast, the Farley building insists on a strict progression through a series of stairs and antechambers that control one's perception of the space. Although the colonnaded wall seems somewhat transparent from the inside, the massive columns succeed in maintaining the separation of interior from exterior.

Another interesting example is the post office in Philadelphia. Constructed as part of the same railroad project twenty-five years later, it also lies opposite the main railroad station. But here, the classical references are much less overt. The colonnade is vestigial: what remains is a contrast between a relatively thin wall and an interior cage. Much of the articulation, proportion, and detailing, however, is certainly reminiscent of the New York building and may well have been intentionally so. With the reduction of its representational content and the emphasis on lightness rather than weight, the Philadelphia post office represents further development toward modern architecture. Miës van der Rohe would complete the process by removing the exterior cladding entirely, expressing only the cage. The simultaneity that is the hallmark of modern design would come not from a contrast in material, but in the overlapping spaces of the building and its plaza.

It is clear from these examples that both classicism and modernism sought perfection in proportion, scale, and finish. Miës's work comes across very well when analyzed in classical terms. The usual distinction of modernism based on use of materials does not apply, and a closer look is needed.

ORGANIZATION

The prototype for classical space is the ancient Roman basilica, where a great central space is surrounded by a series of identical spatial cells. The development of Western architecture can be interpreted in part as a quest for creating the largest possible central space. It is this goal for which the vaulting of High Gothic cathedrals, the domes of Renaissance churches, and the iron spans of nineteenth century exhibition

Figure 15. Main Post Office, Chicago. Ludwig Miës van der Rohe, 1968.

39

HISTORY:
FROM
OLIGARCHY
TO
DEMOCRACY

Figure 16. U. S. post office, Philadelphia. Rankine & Kellog, 1930.

40

Figure 17. Street in San Francisco.

41

HISTORY:
FROM
OLIGARCHY
TO
DEMOCRACY

buildings and railroad stations were developed. The great systems of articulation—Doric, Ionic, Corinthian, and so forth—are based on the support of loads that were intuitive and direct.

Such a great simplification of the history of Western architecture is only meant to distinguish the importance of the hierarchy: a central space served by a system of subsidiary spaces. Efficient construction of this spatial system determined a rectangular grid, apparent in the layout of cities planned under the Roman empire, as well as many of the monastic buildings of the Middle Ages.

During the twentieth century, buildings became a relatively trivial case for structural technology, and the great melodramatic extravaganzas of the Baroque gave way to the pragmatic iron cage. With the development of modernism came an interest in the design of buildings through the incremental addition of planning units, or *modules,* which might be derived from the stretch of an arm, the minimum dimensions of a living space, or a standard structural span. The abstraction of space in modern architecture is a consequence of incrementing a standard module indefinitely. The flatness at the top of International Style skyscrapers is a statement of the arbitrariness of their heights, for they are determined not by structure or esthetics but by economics.

It is just this abstraction that appealed to Frank Lloyd Wright in Japanese architecture, traditionally based on multiples of the *tatami* mat. One result of modular design is a greater interaction with the landscape, since the extension of an abstractly determined module can be projected indefinitely. In Wright's case, he believed that the mathematics that described natural shapes, as in D'Arcy Thompson's *On Growth and Form,* should be applied in architecture as well.

Streets and Site Planning

The development of the commercial city in the nineteenth century was accelerated by the forces of industrialization. Particularly in America, which was a *tabula rasa* as far as the industrialists were concerned, grids of streets were laid out almost without regard to natural features. The art of landscape gardening was applied on a grand scale by experts such as Frederick Law Olmsted, who created Central Park in Manhattan within a perfect rectangle and laid out the influential Columbian Exposition of 1893 in Chicago. This was in a sense a complete reversal of the classical idea of the temple in a fitting natural landscape, for the famous parks of English country houses and the gardens of French *chateaux* were laid out with reference to specific views and orientations determined from an existing center. Central Park was to be a magnificent dream of a Romantic landscape come true in the middle of a commercial city. It does not relate to any particular civic building or complex, although it is entirely enclosed by street walls.

Abstraction of the site planning process develops along with comprehensive zoning regulations, such as that of New York in 1916. Although the intention was to exert a certain degree of control over what seemed to be a chaotic explosion of growth, it also created economic forces, based on the relative value of land, that have come to determine much of the look of the modern city. The economics look good on paper—regardless of the actual return on investment—but when translated into the forms of buildings built under them, there is a lack of comprehensibility. One cannot immediately perceive the forces that generate the forms. Economic laws, although certainly real enough, are not intuitive in the sense that physical laws are. Hence, the loss of tactility in much of modern architecture.

Modern forms of transportation also require a sophisticated level of planning. Many cities and towns in the midwestern United States are based on the location of the railroads that generated much of the development. The requirement for level rights-of-way and grade separation caused huge urban development projects in cities such as New York, Cleveland, Detroit, and Chicago. Later in the twentieth century, vehicular roads and highways brought about another phase of changes.

Cartesian Organization

In classical buildings, the planning grid is used to distinguish the central from the subordinate. In modern buildings, the Cartesian grid is used to generate equivalent modules in three dimensions. The vertical application of a grid is anathematic to classical design in which floor levels reflect social status. But the modern office building requires vertically equivalent floors, made feasible by the development of the elevator. Again, this is an abstraction: one does not *feel* the change in height while traveling in one, and the sensation of vertical progression, so important to classical buildings, is absent.

The application of classical orders to blocks in the city was a characteristic of Beaux-Arts plans such as that for Paris in the 1870s and for many of the neighborhoods in American cities slated for redevelopment for railroad stations. Cleveland and Chicago both include elements of such plans, and perhaps the most famous in the United States is Park Avenue in Manhattan, built above the tracks of the approach to Grand Central Terminal. Colonnade Row in Manhattan was a series of nine speculative houses whose Corinthian colonnade attracted wealthy buyers.

The use of classical styles in the design of office buildings took two forms: application of orderlike details according to the system of base, shaft, and capital; or the stacking of classical temples. The first proved to be easier to work with and many charming examples of this style grace the cities of the United States. However, there is an innate discrepancy between the façade of the building and the regular grid within. The implication of load is patently false, since it is the steel cage that supports the façade, and not the reverse.

Proportion

No issue is more basic to classicism than the proportion of part to part and of part to whole. Elaborate systems of measurements have been developed and disseminated by influential classicists, including Palladio. Such studies were a staple of the Ecole des Beaux-Arts in Paris during the nineteenth and twentieth centuries.

> Proportion is the good breeding of architecture. It is that something, indefinable to the unprofessional eye, which gives repose and distinction to a room: in its origin a matter of nice mathematical calculation, of scientific adjustment of voids and masses, but in its effects as intangible as that all-pervading essence which the ancients called the soul. 8

Edith Wharton's quotation is notable for its compression of so many issues. "Good breeding" implies that design is meant only for certain people, determined by circumstances of birth. "Professional" implies that some people can see things that others cannot. The romanticism of "intangible effects" and the reference to the "ancients" is part of a cult of taste, to be discussed in Chapter 3, Culture: A Change of Scale. The "adjustment of voids and masses" defines the essential classical idea of space as dependent on its enclosure. Mathematics and science are invoked to establish the inevitability of proportion, which can then justify the exclusivity of taste.

The primacy of simple geometric shapes, such as the square, have been problematic in classical architecture because

44

Figure 18. Four remaining houses in Colonnade Row, Manhattan. Seth Geer, 1833.

HISTORY:
FROM
OLIGARCHY
TO
DEMOCRACY

their inflexibility makes planning difficult. A notable example of this is the sixteenth century scheme for St. Peter's church in Rome, where Bramante's perfect square was later enlarged by Maderno to accommodate the masses of pilgrims wishing to visit the church. It is always to be remembered, however, that the richness of the classical system is in its success for resolving such problems. The notion of the Golden Mean, where the shorter side of a rectangle is to the longer side as the longer side is to the whole, gave a useful way of generating rectangular shapes, although, since the proportion does not generate a rational number, it contradicts another classical dictum about using simple, whole-number ratios: 1:2, 1:3, 1:4, and so forth. It has never been persuasively demonstrated that such issues are perceptible by the human eye, professional or not, although myths about sensitivity have always been useful to those seeking power.

So strong is the notion of proportion that modern architects have attempted to develop their own systems, often based on the classical. Le Corbusier's Modulor system is an example of this. But the elemental proportion for modernism remains 1:1, the equivalence of independent elements.

Orientation

The axiality of classical styles establishes a frontal quality in classical buildings. Even where a diagonal approach is allowed, as at Versailles, the final part of the approach is turned perpendicular to the façade. An interesting variation on this theme is Palladio's Villa Rotonda, where the siting and centralization of the building seem to respond to diagonal views.

The frontality of classically designed buildings in modern cities can sometimes be seen to be artificially forced. When Beaux-Arts planning is imposed on blocks divided into privately held parcels, the correctly proportioned scale of one side can appear quite different on the other.

Axiality is supported by symmetry, which was thought for a time in the nineteenth century to be anathema to modern architecture, most notably by William Morris in his designs and John Ruskin in his writings. Edith Wharton responded thus:

> If proportion is the good breeding of architecture, symmetry, or the answering of one part to another, may be defined as the sanity of decoration . . . . As a guide through the byways of art, Mr. Ruskin is entitled to the reverence and gratitude of all; but as a logical exponent of the causes and effects of the beauty he discovers, his authority is certainly open to question . . . .
> What the instinct for symmetry means, philosophers may be left to explain; but that it does exist, that it means something, and that it is most strongly developed in those races which have reached the highest artistic civilization, must be acknowledged by all students of sociology. 9

In fact, it is more characteristic of modern buildings to be symmetrical and asymmetrical simultaneously than to be one or the other. There is innate in human vision a tendency to see symmetrically which can be engaged creatively to suggest simultaneity between dissimilar spaces.

Modern buildings may change in appearance between diagonal and frontal views. A famous example of this is Giuseppe Terragni's *Casa del Fascio* in Como. But many of Wright's buildings from the Prairie period are approached off the axis of bilateral symmetry. Examples include the Darwin Martin House in Buffalo, Unity Temple in Oak Park, and the Hardy House in Racine. Although axes are strongly established, the circulation occurs off the axis, and this dynamic shifting generates a quintessential modern experience of space.

For the modern eye, an unrendered or unfinished side façade may be at least as interesting as a formal, front façade. A change in the nature of the drawing of sections is an indication of this. Beaux-Arts sections tend to render interior elevations in light and shade while indicating solid walls with a simple *poché*. But modern sections must deal with the layers of materials that make up modern construction. Furthermore, modern space conceptualization includes an understanding of layers of space that interact with functional zones in building interiors. Le Corbusier's Villa Stein at Garches is an example of this. The result has been termed "phenomenal transparency" in a famous essay by Colin Rowe and Robert Slutzky:

> stratifications, devices by means of which space becomes constructed, substantial, and articulate, are the essence of that phenomenal transparency which has been noticed as characteristic of the central post-Cubist tradition. 10

This change in how a building is viewed reflects both the greater abstraction that derives from a broadening of knowledge about construction and also a less tactile and more mental perception of the building. The relationship between viewer and building is less controlled in modern buildings, though more inclusive in the sense that a greater range of experience is allowed.

Attitudes toward Nature

Classical buildings of the eighteenth and nineteenth centuries reflect the picturesque view of nature idealized in the art and poetry of the time. The reality of nature, however, was still something to be wary of, and the solid walls of classical buildings served as a psychic as well as physical separation from the natural world.

The modern view of nature was changed by the industrialization of the workplace. With the ability to heat and light artificially in an efficient way, the seasonal cycle became less one of climatic change than of economics. Transparent walls enabled a more direct visual contact with the outdoors from a sheltered environment. The growth of automobile traffic with its concomitant effect on the land around buildings in the form of drives, walks, and parking lots has contributed to the transformation of the perception of nature. The result of all of this is a radically different attitude about buildings and how they fit into their environment.

> In inquiries respecting the laws of the world and the frame of things, the highest reason is always the truest. . . . Empirical science is apt to cloud the sight, and, by the very knowledge of functions and processes, to bereave the student of the manly contemplation of the whole. The savant becomes unpoetic. . . . The American who has been confined, in his own country, to the sight of buildings designed after foreign models, is surprised on entering York Minister [sic] or St. Peter's at Rome, by the feeling that these structures are imitations also,—faint copies of an invisible archetype. 11

Emerson's statement is a sign of a new intellectualization in the perceiving of architecture, derived from a split between the empirical and the ideal. The simultaneous presentation in a work of architecture of these two aspects of design—the mental image and its adaptation to the material conditions of nature—is a hallmark of modernism.

Axiality

Basic to the classical idea of architecture is control of the view and approach. This is achieved by establishing a series of axes, virtual lines through space suggested by the disposition of building elements. The most typical configuration is symmetry, the identity of elements on either side of the primary axis.

The generation of an axis supports a hierarchy of functions designated for the spaces and consequently establishes

48

Figure 19. House on Society Hill, Philadelphia.

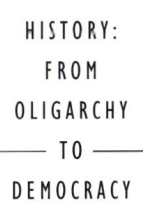

Figure 20. Commercial block in Manhattan.

50

Figure 21. Side wall of loft building, Manhattan.

51

HISTORY:
FROM
OLIGARCHY
TO
DEMOCRACY

Figure 22. Loft building, lower Manhattan.

a social order. The arrangement of rooms *en suite,* or in succession, offers the most control over the sequence of function. This is articulated further by the application of classical orders in various sizes and degrees to the surfaces of walls and surrounding openings such as doors, windows, and fireplaces. The idea of social position is given a more or less direct physical equivalent in the establishment of centrality in classical rooms.

It is commonly thought that the modernist response to classical symmetry is a *dynamic balance,* or the establishment of equality between elements configured differently. Examples of this can certainly be cited, but it is not clear that this is truly the basis for a distinction between the classical and the modern. It would be more precise to say that modern architecture expresses a *dissociation* between the building and its axis. This may be achieved by a collision of separate elements with noncoincident axes of equal emphasis—what is herein termed *disjunctured space.* The recent addition to the Louvre in Paris by I. M. Pei seems quintessentially classical in its exterior manifestation: a perfect quadrilateral pyramid. The precision of its detailing is also in accord with its classical surroundings, although it is in fact a transparent skylight of glass. But its modern content can best be appreciated from a distance, where the prismatic perfection of its surface clearly shows that the orientation of the axis is not perfect and that the entire complex is slightly skewed. The classical design of the Louvre was intended to deny this irregularity; the modern design of the pyramid emphasizes it and adds new meaning to the classical original.

Dissociation between a building and its axis may also be achieved, as is typical of both Frank Lloyd Wright and Le Corbusier, of forcing circulation away from an established axis in a manner that enhances the dissonance. Rather than asymmetry, the typical configuration of a modern building is to be perceived simultaneously as both symmetrical and asymmetrical. There is a lack of resolution about modern buildings that is naturally disturbing. It requires the contribution of an individual's perception to complete the architectural experience. A classical building, on the other hand, is complete in itself, whether anyone is there to see it or not.

Coordination

Perhaps the essential characteristic of the modern vision, a further manifestation of dissociation developed during the nineteenth century: the dissociation between the material reality of a building and one's perception of that reality. Architecture, like literature and music but unlike painting, is perceived sequentially. An impression is built in the mind through memory and intuition as much as through direct perception. Classical architecture confirms and solidifies one's anticipation by generating a complete and comprehensive material reality in which everything follows a strict hierarchical order.

Modern architecture, on the other hand, is not complete without one's perception of it. This is not to say that it is chaotic but that it requires resolution of some sort. Ruskin mentioned this as an aspect of the imagination in *The Seven Lamps of Architecture:*

> The action of the imagination is a voluntary summoning of the conceptions of things absent or impossible. When the imagination deceives it becomes madness. It is a noble faculty so long as it confesses its own ideality; when it ceases to confess this, it is insanity. All the difference lies in the fact of the confession, in there being *no* deception. It is necessary to our rank as spiritual creatures, that we should be able to invent and to behold what is not; and to our rank as moral creatures that we should know and confess at the same time that it is not. 12

Buildings in different classical styles cannot be coordinated, although a variety of them may be pleasing to the eye. They must be seen as separate and unconnected. Modern buildings, on the other hand, can increase in richness as other systems are incorporated. The process of rehabilitation, in fact, can often transform a classically regular building into an interesting modern composite.

Major and minor axes stress the importance of approach in classical buildings. There is a sense of comprehensiveness and order that is alien to the modern experience. Symmetry emphasizes centrality and the importance of position. The Capitol in Washington, D.C., is a highly centralized building, commanding views along the main avenues of the city with its signature dome. But the dome rests not over the seat of government, but over the lobby between the two legislative chambers in the wings. It could be said that the space beneath the dome represents the access of the people to their chosen lawmakers, but this is prevarication. It is interesting that the building program, meant to symbolize the action of popular government in a democracy, seems more suited to a modern solution than with the Late Baroque edifice that was provided. The Houses of Parliament in London resorted to a clock tower at one corner of the Gothic Revival complex. Here, the legislative process is articulated as if it were a business, housed in a series of corridors and rooms relatively indistinguishable from the exterior.

Procession and Movement

The internal configuration of classical buildings developed from series of rooms *en suite*, with movement directed through each in succession, to the provision of separate halls and corridors specifically meant for circulation between and among the functional spaces. At the Ecole des Beaux-Arts in Paris, studies in space planning were based on the provision of appropriate circulation. In fact, a characteristic of Beaux-Arts plans is the relatively enormous amount of area devoted to circulation as compared to other functions. It is fair to assert that, for many Beaux-Arts designers, circulation was considered to be the most important function. The goal of classical design in the nineteenth century and later was to coordinate the functions, including circulation, into a clear and controlled pattern. Movement through even a modest building was to be in this sense processional.

By contrast, movement through a modern building tends to be incidental. Circulation itself is handled as an element that is independent from the other functions of the building. There is a quality of dissociation between occupying the building and moving through it that is both dynamic and unsettling. Many modern architects have expressed interest in the growth of cities, and the concept of the street and what it means has influenced the design of their buildings. One of the finest perceptions of the modern city can be experienced at night along the avenues of Manhattan, where the synchronized traffic lights can be seen as moving bands of alternating red and green. The experience is dynamic and modern.

MODULE

The growth of modern democracy brought about a change in focus from the society to the individual. This transformed the perception of a planning module from that of a generalized building block that could be used to generate larger functional spaces, to that of a more specialized and independent unit, complete in itself. Modern techniques of construction permitted the structure itself to be more or less hidden,

55

HISTORY:
FROM
OLIGARCHY
TO
DEMOCRACY

Figure 23. Classically detailed façades abut without interacting.

Figure 24. The collision of a classically rendered wall with the later expansion of windows enhances the interest of this tower.

and the articulation of the façade became dissociated from it. If classical articulation was used, the spaces behind it could be freely disposed. The suites of apartments in the Haussmann blocks built in the nineteenth century, which are still typical of the avenues of Paris, are an example of this.

When classical articulation seemed unnecessary, the functional units themselves could be expressed. Where flexibility in planning was paramount, this might take the form of undifferentiated transparent bays, as in the famous apartment houses of Ludwig Miës van der Rohe. Although definitively International Style, the articulation of Miës's façades is classical in its reduction of functional differentiation to a purely formal order consistent with the technology of the construction.

The Building Unit

One result of an industrialized construction industry is the replacement of hand crafting by machine production. The cast or carved element becomes a fabricated module, detailed not by the maker but by the designer. The process of design is more and more separated from the process of building, and thus more abstract. The building unit may be a 30-foot by 30-foot steel bay to the structural engineer, an entire floor to the ventilating engineer, a window module to the manufacturer of the curtain wall, and a dwelling unit to the architect. The interaction of these different approaches in the design of a modern building can either result in confusion or architecture.

Precision in construction overcomes plasticity in craft. Stereotomy and casting are modern equivalents of conventional craftsmanship, reflected in the detailing of parts designed for replication. In the modern commercial city, by far the greatest proportion of design work is for buildings that are not to be occupied by the owner. In these cases, economics dictate speed in construction rather than precision, and the detailing of buildings reflects this priority.

The Bay

There is a plastic unity in the classical bay, taller than it is wide. Its proportions are steeped in the tradition of humanism. It has been interpreted by some to reflect the erect stance of the human being, supreme among the creatures of the natural world. Whether this is defensible or not, the unparalleled tactility of classical detailing expresses a closeness and warmth that is frequently missed in modern architecture. The logic of the classical system is restful to the mind in contrast to the dynamism of the modern.

The spatial dynamic of the modern bay, wider than it is long, is a different experience altogether. Louis Sullivan's Carson Pirie Scott store is an example. The articulation of the classical wall is reduced to the flatness of the modern partition. The independence of the space from structure makes the appearance of a column no more than an incident.

The Functional Unit

During the industrialization of the nineteenth century, there was a change in the relationship between leisure and work. The prototypes for most classical buildings, the church-temple and the palace or villa were no longer appropriate models for the developing world. Instead, the office building, factory, and individual residence became the generative functional prototypes for buildings. The office building and factory gained importance through the growth of the commercial city. With the ability to operate continuously regardless of season or weather, these workplaces were more and more determined by the mechanical systems and equipment that had been developed to allow nonstop work. In the home, an increase in the proportion of white-collar and professional

workers called for residences that could be maintained without live-in servants. With the development of modern plumbing, the kitchen moved into the house and became a livable room.

In both cases, interior rooms were laid out and furnished with attention to the functions to be performed in them rather than to the status of the occupant. Wall space was needed for storage, which came to be built into the walls, and for lighting, provided through windows of new design. Ceilings were configured for artificial light and ventilation. There was a great reduction in built-in finishing, and a concomitant growth in commercial decorating supplies.

The importance of the auditorium in modern times is equivalent to the forum and temple of classic times. Studies in the sciences of acoustics and light control enabled these structures to be tailored for different types of performances. Their appearance became more abstract, dependent on mathematical principles unfamiliar to the audience and therefore lacking in the clarity of the classical system.

The Seagram Building

Although long considered an archetype of the International Style, and thus of modernism itself, Ludwig Miës van der Rohe's masterpiece is also an interesting example of the classical content of modernism. When it was first constructed, it provided an open plaza on a street lined solidly with classically detailed business and residential blocks that dated from the development of the Grand Central Terminal fifty years before. The contrast was almost universally applauded and so startling that a revision in the New York City Zoning Resolution encouraged the construction of similar towers situated on street-level plazas.

As a result, most of the neighboring blocks were replaced by International Style towers of indifferent quality, although the Seagram Building remains distinctive through its detailing, proportion, and clarity of massing. These are all, of course, classical virtues and the practice of using modern materials in a classical composition that is so characteristic of many International Style buildings raises the question of the modern content of such buildings.

The Seagram Building is an extreme example because the metal in its curtain wall is bronze rather than aluminum or steel. Bronze was selected at great expense to allow for sharp arrises and shadow lines, lending a classical surface richness and tactility that is notoriously absent in other International Style buildings. Here is a monumental edifice, intended to represent a business corporation, symmetrically disposed and axially oriented. It is detailed with precision to express the clarity and organization of its component parts. What makes it modern?

If modernism is defined by building materials, then it is technology rather than esthetics that determines style. There must be a distinctively modern content to justify modern style, and in the case of the Seagram Building, that content is most perceivable at the plaza level. For it is here that the transparency of the curtain wall allows a most nonclassical continuity of the plaza with the lobby. The difference between the ground level, evenly surfaced throughout in travertine, and the office floors suspended above is expressed as strongly as the distinction between inside and out. One is played up while the other has been played down to achieve the dissociation characteristic of modernism. This is enhanced by the clarity of the elevator shafts which balance the travertine elements with the bronze in a dynamic way. Neither controls the other.

It is characteristic of Miës van der Rohe's work that its

Figure 25. Seagram Building, New York.
Ludwig Miës van der Rohe, 1958.

HISTORY:
FROM
OLIGARCHY
TO
DEMOCRACY

classical content elucidates the progression of modern thinking. His buildings have an element of timelessness that is accompanied by a specifically modern interpretation of what contemporary classicism must be. The modern content lies in the spatial relationships, not in the materials.

The loss of impact that occurred when the Seagram's neighbors were remade in its image, more or less, is characteristic of modernism. Classical buildings are meant to work together if they are properly designed. The planning of Park Avenue early in the twentieth century over the new railroad terminal below was a model of Beaux-Arts consistency.

Modern buildings, on the other hand, work best alone, as contrasting elements in the classical continuum. The stretch of Rockefeller Center along Sixth Avenue, just three blocks west of the Seagram Building in Manhattan, is a typical example of International Style planning. Its public plazas front a series of separated tower slabs with the minimal detailing characteristic of the style. In spite of the popularity of the public spaces, the buildings are indifferent *en masse*, expressing no conviction about scale, proportion, or any other humanist idea. The importance of contrast for modernism stems from its origins as a denial of classicism. It includes the design principles of classical buildings, but it rejects the authoritarian implications of strict hierarchy. When there are few classical elements visible to deny, the impact becomes cerebral rather than visual, and something is lost.

Sacred Places

Just as a truly democratic government inevitably denies a classically proportioned social hierarchy, the tradition of freedom of religion has resulted in a great transformation of the position of churches. In America, churches became a specialized form of auditorium, partly because of the oratorical nature of the various sects common in the colonies. Congregations typically had the greatest say in how their churches were to be run, rather than a centralized hierarchy, and this resulted in a devaluation of traditional religious symbolism in church buildings.

Consider the importance of churches in Italy, where a church would command a square and be the center of a neighborhood. Then contrast with this the example of New Haven, Connecticut, whose centerpiece is three churches of similar sizes but different styles that neighbor each other on the green. The expression of equivalence rather than hierarchy required the development of styles beyond the classical.

In Charles Bulfinch's Meeting House built in Lancaster, Massachusetts, in 1813–14, one can discern—with the benefit of a trained modern eye—prototypical qualities that would appear at the core of modern architecture a hundred years later. This is not to say that Bulfinch anticipated modernism but that the architectonic qualities he so skillfully dealt with in this building are those that struck later eyes as significant in the changing world. In this simple building, one can readily see, for example, premonitions of the work of Louis Kahn.

What is so striking is the way that the building articulates itself as one moves from the frontal view to the diagonal. The arches of the portico—even today breathtaking in simplicity—which appear to encase the thin wooden pilasters are revealed to be delicate, even diaphanous, when their thickness becomes visible. A dialogue is raised between the arcuated supporting structure of the brick and the trabeated supporting structure of the wood, an expression so precisely balanced that neither dominates. This dialogue is emphasized by the almost total lack of ornament. The craft of sculpture and woodworking is here replaced by the craft of building.

It is worth mentioning that this interplay between two structural systems is one of the most characteristic of classi-

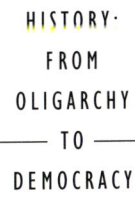

HISTORY·
FROM
OLIGARCHY
TO
DEMOCRACY

Figure 26. Old Meeting House, Lancaster, Massachusetts. Charles Bulfinch, 1813–14.

Figure 27. Old Meeting House, Lancaster, Massachusetts. Charles Bulfinch, 1813–14.

63

HISTORY·
FROM
OLIGARCHY
TO
DEMOCRACY

Figure 28. Massachusetts State House, Boston. Charles Bulfinch, 1793–95.

cal motifs, deriving from the Roman triumphal arch. It is one of the hallmarks of Renaissance architecture and can be found in Michelangelo's Capitol in Rome as well as in the neoclassical architecture of Palladio. It is about the resolution of hierarchy and scale, the smaller assisting the larger, the coordination of detail. In the classical system, a giant trabeated order is articulated by a lesser order, coordinated with it, and frequently by a third suborder in the form of decorative window and door surrounds. The clarity of such a system depends on the skill with which the designer arranges the parts *according to a well-defined classical system of hierarchy.* Thus, the Doric supports the Ionic which, in turn, supports the Corinthian. There is plenty of room for flexibility and variation in the classical system, even reversal or denial, but the notion of hierarchy is never violated.

In the Lancaster Meeting House, however, there is a sense of independence of the structural systems. It almost seems as if two separate designs, one trabeated and one arcuated, were superimposed on each other without adjustment. There is a tension here that is completely unlike the classical expression of repose more typical of neoclassical buildings, such as Bulfinch's own Massachusetts State House, conceived for the capitol about twenty years before the Lancaster church.

It comes as no surprise that the historical development of architectural styles over the past two hundred years includes both a classical and a modern strain. The modern can be associated with the growth of democratic societies, as the classic in its nineteenth century codification is associated first with the declining empires of Europe and later with new authoritarian regimes. In fact, in Italy, Germany, and Russia in the 1920s and 1930s, the modernist styles then current lost favor to classicism as the respective regimes grew more autocratic.

Significantly, the current debate in architecture centers on the distinction between modern and classical. The continuing technological revolution of modern society casts doubt on all certainties and may be expected to have a major influence over architectural styles indefinitely.

Chapter 2
TECHNOLOGY: ABSTRACTION OF KNOWLEDGE

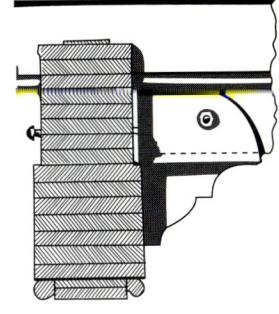

The issue of technological change has always been at the heart of the distinction between classical and modern architectural design. In the examination of the Seagram Building and the Main Post Office in Chicago, it was pointed out that Ludwig Miës van der Rohe applied to modern construction materials a clarity of detail and proportion that was quintessentially classical and that produced modern spaces. His work is the best demonstration that modernism includes classicism in a critical way. The criticism has to do with the substantiality of classical form, its dependence on a simple opposition of solid and void and the importance of sensing gravity kinesthetically. Modern construction is not massive but lightweight. It is assembled from systems of prefabricated components that can occupy the same place at the same time. When this simultaneity is expressed as a *coordination* of building systems, as in Miës's work, it repeats the classical hierarchy of order and harmony.

It is when the building systems are expressed as *independent* that the modern idea of disjunctured space is attained. This does not mean a chaotic jumble of independent shapes and spaces, or a trivial expressionism. The integrity of the modern vision must be expressed through the integrity of the systems that are put together to make the whole. The systems—curtain wall, masonry, steel frame, lighting, functional spaces, roof—must be seen to retain their independence from each other.

This approach to design presupposes a sophisticated understanding of technology. The enormous increase in technical knowledge that accompanied the industrialization of Western societies in the nineteenth century increased the impact of science on culture. Every field of endeavor was abstracted, categorized, and formalized. This was the vision of the Enlightenment of the eighteenth century, and it is part of the classical view of the universe.

But the classicists sought harmony and a comprehensive order, equivalent to divine law, that encompassed all knowledge. The rate at which technology has advanced since the Enlightenment has been so rapid that a comprehensive knowledge of science, once considered essential for a cultured gentleman, is impossible. Although the laws of Isaac Newton

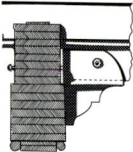

in physics are commonly taught in secondary schools, advanced physics today depends on concepts so far removed from everyday perception that even highly educated individuals have difficulty understanding them. Yet the results of modern physics are present everywhere—in electronic devices, the production of nuclear energy, and so forth.

Two aspects of this change have determined the nature of modern understanding. One is a view found in *On Growth and Form,* a seminal work by the British zoologist D'Arcy Thompson:

> In Aristotle's parable, the house is there that men may live in it; but it is also there because the builders have laid one stone upon another. It is as a *mechanism,* or a mechanical construction, that the physicist looks upon the world. 1

The mechanistic view is overt in Le Corbusier's conception of the house as *une machine d'habiter* but is also the basis for Wright's interest in the organic. Frequently confused with functionalism, organic architecture in fact derived its forms from the idea of growth in nature. D'Arcy Thompson's seminal work, in addition to that of many others, showed that natural shapes such as those found in leaves, trees, and animals resulted from the regular growth of simple geometric patterns. Thus, when the dimension of time is added to classical geometry, a new range of shapes is derived. It is such shapes that were termed *organic* by Wright and others.

The way to understand the modern world is technical rather than spiritual. The secularization of modern society is a direct result of the expansion of science into areas that had previously been the domain of faith. Darwin's *Origin of Species* is of course the most famous example, but it is only one blow of a massive assault on the nature of belief. Intuition has been devalued, not only in the general advance of science but by psychology as well. Faith and belief can themselves be studied, categorized, and assigned a value.

All of this is expressed in the design of buildings that are generated solely through intellectual rather than intuitive means. Aldo Rossi's influential *The Architecture of the City* and Christian Norberg-Schulz's *Genius Loci: Towards a Phenomenology of Architecture* are among the many critical works that seek to restore a sense of intuition to architecture. That they attempt this through scientific means—observation and deduction—is symptomatic of the modern dilemma.

SPACE

Classical space is directly determined by its enclosing masses. The duality of solid and void characteristic of masonry construction is essential to classical architecture. The effect of good classical design is a harmony between the visual and the tactile senses.

In the modern era, the link between size and weight has been broken. Enormous structures are built as lightly as possible. There is a loss of tangibility in modern design that is a result of the change from a modeled architecture to a layered architecture. Modern architecture is constructed from systems that are prefabricated into components that are essentially planar, or two-dimensional, and then assembled at the site in layers. Contemporary construction techniques are economically driven, and the layering of construction systems allows successive crews of specialized laborers to complete their work in the quickest possible time.

Lacking the clarity of the solid-void duality, modern architecture calls for a higher level of participation from the viewer. Perception of a modern space requires an act of reconstruction in the mind, a process of interpretation of incomplete or ambiguous material cues to perceive a spatial continuum that is only partially generated in three-dimensional space. This is why modern architectural criticism speaks of colliding spaces, virtual planes, transparency, and similar mental constructs.

An important element in modern construction is the way in which buildings are produced. Many critical studies compare drawings of modern and classical buildings, analyzing their plans or elevation. Until the nineteenth century, however, very few construction drawings were actually produced for a building. Much of the actual design took place in the stoneworker's shop or at the site. Many contemporary engravings were done after completion of the building.

During the nineteenth century, the techniques of drafting expanded as paper became cheaper. The two-dimensional planning of buildings as taught at the Ecole des Beaux-Arts codified classical design and generated a new way of describing proposed buildings. The flatness of modern architecture is a consequence of a two-dimensional means of design. The later work of Le Corbusier was an attempt to regain the tectonic quality of classical architecture, moving away from the thin planarity of his early work.

Enclosure

In contrast to the classical archetype, modern space is no longer defined entirely by enclosing surfaces. An early example of a very sophisticated modern space can be found at Henry Hobson Richardson's Old Colony Railroad station at North Easton, Massachusetts. Here, the edge of the roof at the approach defines a T-shaped prism while the free-standing wall with its arch layers the space in a rectangle distinct from the interior of the station. The placing of this arch so that its springing points are offset from those of the station arches behind increases its independence from the station system. The sheltering element, the great roof, is clearly distinguished from the enclosing walls.

The course of brownstone that reads as a continuous band just above head height is repeated inside the station in oak. It intersects the arch of the window in a manner that reinforces its independence from the masonry structure. This motif appears in the work of Frank Lloyd Wright ten years later. It also can be found in early steel-frame buildings, where the expression of the masonry wall is independent of the interior frame. In the Judge Building by McKim, Mead & White, the façade on the side street is more interesting to modern eyes than the classically articulated front on Fifth Avenue. The depth of the reveal and the plainness of the cut emphasize the tactile quality of the masonry contrasted with the light interior frame.

The idea of enclosure itself has changed from its classical sense, which included a strong element of protectiveness. Modern space is delimited to define a functional activity, and the enclosure can be any of a variety of types. The light weight of modern construction allows the support of a ceiling to be denied entirely. The modular nature of modern buildings implies an unlimited extension of space. Virtual spaces can be generated in the mind through architectural features that suggest lines and planes. Such spaces can overlap or contradict each other, bringing about a sensation of dynamism that is completely foreign to the classical ideal.

Walls as Support

In classical design, the surface defines volume. Walls, piers, and columns are solid and heavy. The construction of arches and domes depends on the weight of the mass of masonry that prevents the *voussoirs* from collapsing. One's sense of this weight is part of the essential experience of classical

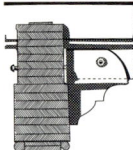

68

Figure 29. Old Colony Railroad Station, North Easton, Massachusetts. Henry Hobson Richardson, 1881–82.

architecture. The fitness, the rightness of a classical building has much to do with one's ability to intuit the integrity of its structure. The basis for classical decoration is the articulation of structural parts derived from those of ancient times. The weight of the building is perceived as part of the force of gravity, an unchanging downward pull.

But in the modern world, the idea of weight has become separated from the idea of size and scale. Airships were an early twentieth century example of massive objects that were weightless. Perceiving such objects requires an intellectual resolution of something that seems impossible. Direct intuition must be replaced with an abstract construct of some sort.

The invention of steel and reinforced concrete construction methods have transformed the classical idea of solid balanced against gravity. In Paul Rudolph's building for the Government Services Center in Boston, massive concrete beams slide past great fluted piers rather than resting on them. In this way, the steel reinforcing bars embedded in the concrete can be perceived through intuition: they are an essential missing part that must be supplied by the mind in order to comprehend how the building is supported. This manner of engaging perception by presenting an incompletely elucidated structure is characteristic of modern systems.

Reinforcing had begun to be part even of classical buildings by the nineteenth century. With the advances in construction techniques, arches and colonnades were reduced to decorative elements. The James J. Farley post office in Manhattan built in 1912 is a steel-framed structure with a classically correct colonnade that happens to be perched above a major railroad terminal, as was the original Pennsylvania Station across the street. Many noble civic and governmental structures have been constructed with classical colonnades.

For modern buildings, there is the problem of revealing structure in a tectonic way to express function when the support of modern lightweight buildings is relatively trivial.

At the Richard Hughes Justice Complex in Trenton, New Jersey, this question was addressed through the use of a monumental truss system to suspend the Supreme Courtroom of New Jersey above a public plaza. The approach to the courtroom is across a bridge that penetrates the truss members themselves. This is equivalent to the monumental stair and colonnade at the approach to the Supreme Court of the United States in Washington, D.C.

The clear separation of structural support and layered panels is one of the main design themes of the Hughes Complex. Another is the separation of circulation between the public and the staff. The expression of independent systems results in a modern space that is nevertheless strongly centralized.

Frames

The articulation of the wall in a classical building is meant to express a masonry structure of trabeated and arcuated systems coordinated for stability. At the church of Il Redentore in Venice, Palladio's nave is a model of repose. The major and minor systems are perfectly related in proportion to each other, and the structural support of the load of the main vault can be readily traced down through the members to the ground. The depth of relief of the members is coordinated with their importance.

In modern architecture, the framing of masonry systems as reinforced concrete, poured as a liquid into molds, is entirely different. The connections between horizontal and vertical members are designed for rigidity, which is in a certain sense a combination of the effects of trabeated and arcu-

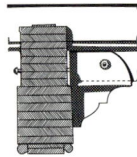

70

Figure 30. Old Colony Railroad Station, North Easton, Massachusetts. Henry Hobson Richardson, 1881–82.

71

TECHNOLOGY:
ABSTRACTION
— OF —
KNOWLEDGE

Figure 31. Judge Building, Manhattan.
McKim, Mead & White, 1888.

Figure 32. Goodyear blimp.

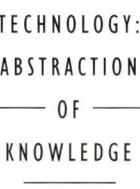

TECHNOLOGY:
ABSTRACTION
OF
KNOWLEDGE

Figure 33. Boston Government Service Center. Paul Rudolph, 1962–71.

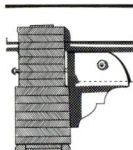

74

Figure 34. Richard Hughes Justice Complex, Trenton. The Grad Partnership, 1979.

75

TECHNOLOGY:
ABSTRACTION
OF
KNOWLEDGE

Figure 35. Il Redentore, Venice. Palladio, 1577.

Figure 36. Baker House, Massachusetts Institute of Technology. Alvar Aalto, 1947–48.

76

Figure 37. Hallidie Building, San Francisco. Willis Polk, 1917.

ated systems. Rigid frames are less directly perceptible than classical systems. At Baker House, Alvar Aalto expressed a rectilinear concrete frame directly. It turns in response to the undulating plan, and circulation is along the axis of the bays as in the Palladian church. But Aalto's structure seems to be twisted and stretched in response to circulation, quite unlike the classical building's strict progression through the structural members.

Membranes

Primitive architecture can be generally divided into two structural prototypes, the tent and the cave. Framed architecture developed from the tent prototype of some kind of membrane or infill supported on a wooden structure. Arcuated architecture developed from the cave prototype of a space tunneled out of a mass of stone. When the early wooden temples of the Greeks were memorialized in stone, the membrane became a relatively trivial element in Western architecture. It became important again in the age of the High Gothic cathedrals in the form of stained-glass windows. But in classical architecture, windows remained openings in solid masonry rather than elements of a membrane system.

In its rejection of the classical tradition, early modernists turned again to primitive sources of design, newly available through archaeological studies. The tent was again thought of as a prototype for glass walls, rendered as membranes stretched over an independent internal supporting frame. Frank Lloyd Wright overtly explored tent prototypes in several projects. But the connection of the membrane idea with advances made in suspension supporting systems for bridges resulted in experimental structural systems such as the terminal for Dulles Airport by Eero Saarinen. The building is classically oriented, symmetrical in relation to its control tower. The supporting pylons are proportioned and ranked like a classical colonnade. But the roof is visibly hung above the great room of the terminal, and the curved glazing between the columns enhances the reading of it as a membrane. The Dulles terminal, like Lincoln Center, employs modern materials in a classical manner. But its spatial concept is much clearer, and the distinction between its classical and modern elements is pointed rather than confused.

Outside and Inside

Classical architecture was an international style. It combined the trabeated, beam-and-column prototype (tent) of the Greek temple with the arcuated masonry wall (cave) of the Romans into a flexible, coherent system that could be applied in any climate. The two structural models remained distinct and the variety of combinations thus made possible provided the empire builders of western Europe with an excellent means of articulating a centralized, hierarchical social order. Just as the sculptures, paintings, and figured windows of the great medieval cathedrals were used to educate an illiterate public, the representation of the classical orders—hierarchically valued from Tuscan to Composite—reinforced the ideal of a closed, controlled society in which everyone had an assigned part to play. The representation was more subtle in its reference to a supposed Golden Age of the past which only the educated could really appreciate.

Resistance to the classical standard typically took the form of a search for structural integrity, that is, the exposure of actual supporting members accurately expressing their functions. John Ruskin staked a claim for Gothic Revival in terms that would later be used by early modernists:

> Architectural deceits are broadly to be considered under three heads:—

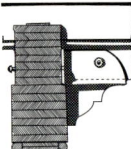

> 1st. The suggestion of a mode of structure or support, other than the true one; as in pendants of late Gothic roofs.
>
> 2d. The painting of surfaces to represent some other material than that of which they actually consist (as in the marbling of wood), or the deceptive representation of sculptured ornament upon them.
>
> 3d. The use of cast or machine-made ornaments of any kind. 2

As the framing of buildings become more and more trivial in terms of weight, the expression of structure lost much of its intrinsic impact upon architecture. The most important function of the wall changed from support to enclosure. The availability of large sizes of glass enabled the visual sense of inside/outside to act independently of the physical separation. The challenge to the classical system was to include what had been outside: new forms, shapes, and ideas brought about by technological change in the developing western societies. The absurdity of the revivalist approach in a modern world could occasionally take direct physical form, as in the notorious combination of Georgian and Gothic styles at Yale University. The problem is not so much the combination as that it doesn't seem to make much of a difference to the design.

Modern architects sought to break the exclusivity innate in classical styles and began to pay more attention to the process by which a building was made. That this was a gradual process in the United States is suggested by the difficulty historians have had in designating the first skyscraper. A series of business buildings in downtown Chicago in the 1880s and 1890s incrementally reduced the supporting function of the masonry street façade as the interior frames were designed to take more and more of the load.

The question of structural integrity remained throughout the development of modernism, resulting in an expressionist strain that can be seen in the works of such architects as Eero Saarinen, Jörn Utzon, and Paul Rudolph. When structural support is trivial as a technical point, expression of structure requires extreme gestures, an operatic intensity that can only be justified by the individual result. Robert Venturi, Denise Scott-Brown, and Steven Izenour were alluding to this in their influential *Learning From Las Vegas*:

> We shall emphasize image—image over process or form—in asserting that architecture depends in its perception and creation on past experience and emotional association and that these symbolic and representational elements may often be contradictory to the form, structure, and program with which they combine in the same building. 3

The International Style skyscraper expresses the truth about structure innately. Its flat top implies that height is not a structural issue; more or less could have been built. At the U.S. Steel Building in Manhattan, Skidmore, Owings and Merrill managed to comply with fireproofing regulations while exposing the outer face of structural steel I-beams, but this has little impact on the overall design, except for a tactile richness unusual for the International Style.

Tempered Interiors

Tempering of interiors allows full-time, year-round occupation of the building. The intellectualization of knowledge that accompanied industrialization had inevitably brought to architecture, as well as the other arts, an abstraction that many experienced as cold and indifferent. But the tempered interior behind its sealed windows led to a deeper abstraction: one of time itself whereby the natural process of seasonal change had less and less effect on human endeavors.

79

TECHNOLOGY:
ABSTRACTION
OF
KNOWLEDGE

Figure 38. Dulles Airport, Chantilly, Virginia. Eero Saarinen, 1958–62.

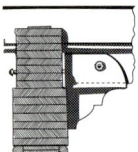

80

81

TECHNOLOGY: ABSTRACTION OF KNOWLEDGE

Figure 39. Davenport College, Yale University.

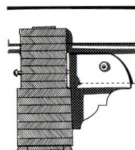

Figure 40. U.S. Steel building, Manhattan. Skidmore, Owings and Merrill, 1965.

Solid and Void

Classical architecture is hard-edged and clear. Its supreme method of construction, masonry, determined the proportions of walls and their openings, although the basis for much of classical detailing was the idealized wooden temples of the early Greeks. The duality of solid and void that is a concomitant feature of masonry supported clarity over ambiguity. Architects such as Vanbrugh, Soane, and Lutyens were able to invest the classical ideal with an element of ambiguity by using classical elements and proportions in a self-contradicting manner that modern architects have found to be a rich source of inspiration.

Modern construction separates weight from solidity. The lightness of modern construction allows walls that are both solid and transparent at the same time. The conviction conveyed by classical solids in daylight rendered by shadows has been replaced by the ambiguity of changing transparency, virtual space, and artificial lighting both inside and out.

Wind and Pressure

Just as necessary to the development of modern skyscrapers as structural engineering is an understanding of the tempering of air for ventilation. This has more to do with modern design than the expression of mechanical systems, for the gradual building of knowledge over the centuries since the classical age resulted in a radically different concept of the atmosphere of the planet we inhabit. That a substance essential to life was colorless, odorless, tasteless, and virtually weightless but could nevertheless be understood and experienced was an idea that has had a lot to do with the abstract conception of space, a notion quite different from that of the classical void. For space in the modern sense is not completely determined by that which surrounds or encloses it. It has characteristics of its own that affect its enclosure to a degree equivalent to the converse.

The accumulation of technological knowledge that has brought about the modern idea of space is not limited to the science of atmospheric gases. The rationalization of wind pressure and its effects on tall buildings and the studies of circulation within public buildings have also contributed to the conception. Thus, the modern idea of space is dynamic rather than static. Space is seen as a field of forces that must be accommodated by the structure and envelope of the building and that determine the form of that envelope to a large degree.

Classical architecture developed from the necessity to resolve a single force: weight. Its vocabulary of structural shapes—the column, the wall, the arch, and the dome—are derived from that process of resolution. Modern architecture does not seek to resolve but to balance a collection of dynamic forces that are mutually independent into a complex whole which itself includes the resolution of structure.

> The form . . . of any portion of matter, whether it be living or dead, and the changes of form which are apparent in its movement and in its growth, may in all cases alike be described as due to the action of force. In short, the form of an object is a "diagram of forces," in this sense, at least, that from it we can judge of or deduce the forces that are acting or have acted upon it. . . . In an organism, great or small, it is not merely the nature of the *motions* of the living substance which we must interpret in terms of force (according to kinetics), but also the *conformation* of the organism itself, whose permanence or equilibrium is explained by the interaction or balance of forces, as described in statics. 4

The dynamism inherent in the modern world brought attention to spaces formed by movement, mostly from systems of transportation. This includes the forms of roads and bridges, which more and more became dominant forms on the landscapes of Western cities, and also includes spaces

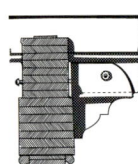

Figure 41. Highways near Los Angeles. *Ca.* 1960.

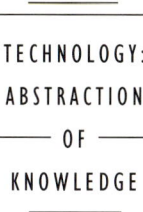

85

TECHNOLOGY:
ABSTRACTION
— OF —
KNOWLEDGE

Figure 42. Railroad coach interior. *Ca.* 1910.

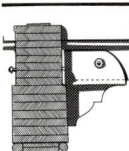

such as the interior of railroad coaches, whose linear organization reflected the dynamic of the machine age. The expression of motion was a natural concomitant to the simultaneity of independent systems, which itself involved an element of time as well as space.

GEOMETRY

Classical geometry, derived from ancient Euclidean geometry and Cartesian geometry of the seventeenth century, is based on the rigorous definition of geometric shapes by mathematical formulas. This essentially closed system was transformed by the development of modern mathematics beginning in the eighteenth century. The new ability to describe surfaces and shapes beyond the basic conic sections in three-dimensional space allowed a mathematically precise description of complex forms such as the intersection of curved roofs. Mechanized prefabrication depends on the accurate description of such shapes.

Another important application of geometry in modern times is its use in advanced mathematical analysis. Beginning with analytic geometry, founded by René Descartes, it was shown that algebraic computation could be derived from geometric quantification. This enabled the calculation of, for example, stress concentration in structures. The trend was for architectural applications to become a relatively trivial application of the advanced geometrical methods used in such fields as thermodynamics and fluid dynamics.

Classical concepts such as that of the Golden Mean lost ground as geometry expanded to include dimensions above the three necessary to describe space. The geometric foundation of architecture became more abstract at the same time that it was trivialized from the point of view of advanced mathematics.

Cartesian Solids

The geometry that is the basis for classical architecture is itself founded upon the most basic shapes that can be generated by points, lines, and planes. These shapes include the sphere, the cylinder, the cube, the cone, and the regular pyramid. In their purest forms, they are of limited utility for buildings, the rectangular parallelepiped being typical for architecture. Although the Cartesian solids were frequently put to use as decorative elements, in the late eighteenth century the architects Ledoux and Boulée devised highly theoretical designs for grandiose structures based firmly upon them.

The result, for classicism, is an architecture of reason that is strongly hierarchical in essence. The assembly of simple shapes results in composite structures of great lucidity. The simplicity of the Cartesian solids lies in their mathematics, for they are not easy to carve or to shape. Construction of the Perisphere at the New York World's Fair of 1939 involved complicated, custom-formed steel members and furnaced plates. The Cartesian solids are, however, easy to draw in two dimensions. It is not surprising that classical buildings are more readily drawn than, for example, Gothic buildings, whose effect is best transmitted through paintings or renderings.

Simplicity for modernists includes the modularity of fabrication. The techniques of industrialization are best suited to assemblies of rectangular proportion. Where they are used, higher-order curves such as the hyperboloid, catenary, or parabola appear as well as those based on the circle. The triangulation of structural trusses has added a diagonal element to modern design that is foreign to classicism. The interaction of diagonals with rectilinear building systems is a recurring theme in modern design.

87

TECHNOLOGY:
ABSTRACTION
OF
KNOWLEDGE

Figure 43. Interaction of highways. The newer road below is delicately bent to avoid the upper trestle's heavy trusswork, which is poised lightly on concrete piers.

Ornamentation versus Abstraction

The neoclassical architecture of the early nineteenth century was a monochrome version of ancient multicolored models. It represented in stone details derived from wooden structures. The resulting styles were an abstract idea of Western culture, well suited to transmission by two-dimensional drawings and favored by the ruling classes of European countries.

With the industrialization of building materials, an even higher level of abstraction was generated. Cast and pressed copies could be made from handmade originals. The representation of actual building components such as fasteners and joints brought about a new conception of ornamentation: that which was integral to the construction and that which was decorative. The famous dictum of the early modernist Adolf Loos that ornament is a crime is related to the notion of expressing structural necessity.

Techniques in Drawing and Design

The industrialization of paper making, supported by the vast forests of North America, advanced the quantity and technical quality of architectural drawings. The publication of measured drawings of the ruins at Pompeii and Herculaneum late in the eighteenth century began a series of bound collections of architectural drawings of existing buildings. The availability of paper enabled the efficient production and circulation of pattern-books.

Coupled with the advances in descriptive geometry, these developments supported the growth of technical drawing. Tightened and codified at the Ecole des Beaux-Arts, standard plans, elevations, and sections were expanded by axonometric and perspective renderings, detail drawings, and independent structural and mechanical drawings.

With the invention of perspective the modern notion of individualism found its artistic counterpart. Every element in a perspective representation is related to the unique point of view of the individual spectator. 5

Almost all of these drawings were monochrome, reproduced where necessary by engraving techniques. The teaching of skills in rendering and *poché* emphasized classical buildings as abstract, modeled surfaces in light and shade, consisting of solid masses and voids.

The twentieth century saw great technological advances in the reproduction of drawings. The standard set of building plans was becoming highly specialized, with rendered visualizations optional. The analytical, abstract quality of modern buildings depends in part on the way they are conceived. Not only has drafting become codified to the point where many builders can understand their working drawings only with difficulty, but the separation of building trades into separate sets of drawings has contributed to the modern sense of space as a composite of independent elements.

The Intellectualization of the Arch

The arch as a structural element was developed by the Romans to span large spaces in masonry. The vault and the dome are expansions of the arch principle over larger spaces. The development of the idea of an arch has been suggested by some historians as a measure of the development of a civilization, for instance, in the temples of the Mayan civilization of seventh century Mexico. There, although vaults were approached in form, the idea of a keystone and wedge-shaped blocks, or *voussoirs*, to transmit the load appears not to have been experimented with. It is notable that Western scholars have often judged the achievements of other civilizations as more or less incomplete attainments of the European ideal.

TECHNOLOGY: ABSTRACTION OF KNOWLEDGE

Figure 44. Metro station, Washington, D.C.

Figure 45. Ames Library, North Easton, Massachusetts. Henry Hobson Richardson, 1877–79.

91

TECHNOLOGY:
ABSTRACTION
—— OF ——
KNOWLEDGE

Figure 46. Interior detail. Entrance of Ames Library.

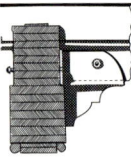

Vaulted spaces in modern architecture are rarely structural, since the masonry, even when detailed according to classical principles, is more efficiently carried by a steel frame. Such monuments as McKim, Mead & White's Municipal Building in lower Manhattan, its entrance arch detailed to follow Michelangelo's Farnese Palace in Rome, are examples of this. There are still cases, however, when structural vaulting is used, primarily in tunnels or other subgrade applications. The vaulted subway stations for the Metro in Washington, D.C., are formed from modular concrete panels, which clearly express the lightness and prefabrication of modern design rather than the pressure of immense weight. The development of arches into thin-shell reinforced concrete vaults specifically denies the defining characteristic of the classical arch: weight locking itself in place.

When the structural principles behind the arch were made superfluous by the development of metal-framed architecture, it was the opening rather than the structure that took on the symbolism associated with the arch. In the later years of the nineteenth century, Henry Hobson Richardson's architecture detailed arched openings with dramatic oversized voussoirs just at the time when they were no longer technologically relevant. This can be sensed through the relative independence of the wall that the arch cuts. From the porch of the Ames library, the arch seems lighter and more delicate than from the exterior.

Richardson's architecture is an example of a revival style beginning to generate some of the principles that would later define modern architecture. For example, the separation of opening and screen—the discontinuity between shape and structure—is readily apparent in the façade of his Crane Memorial Library. The openings are defined by the various functions within the library: reading room, offices, and entrance. Their position in the wall is not axially related to the overall shape but is configured in a way that implies a second axis, equal in weight to the other. The flatness of the masonry and abstraction of the stonework have a diagrammatic quality that invokes the drawings from which they were built. There is an equivalency of readings—the structure, the function, the historic references, the design drawings—that blend to give a very modern impression in this sophisticated design.

Plasticity

The tectonic quality of classical architecture is successfully captured in Richardson's architecture. There is not yet the sense of layered panels lightly joined that is more characteristic of later modern work. He achieved this not just through the contrast between rustication and flatness, but also with carefully wrought edges at corners and joints. This required manual skills that were to disappear in the twentieth century.

Modern design is assembled rather than carved. Parts are attached rather than joined in the sense of carpentry or masonry. One of the results of the industrialization of construction has been the creation of new industries in fasteners and sealants. Economically driven, contemporary design seeks to minimize time spent at the job site by providing standardized components that can easily be assembled with tools that require little training to use.

Coordination of Systems

The work of Miës van der Rohe demonstrates the potential for a classical expression using modern materials. This supports John Summerson's contention:

> Technological progress has really very little to do with advances in architectural design and it is by no means true that the "new materials" of our time have changed archi-

93

TECHNOLOGY:
ABSTRACTION
OF
KNOWLEDGE

Figure 47. Crane Memorial Library, Quincy, Massachusetts. H.H. Richardson, 1880–83.

Figure 48. Entrance, Crane Memorial Library, Quincy, Massachusetts. H.H. Richardson, 1880–83.

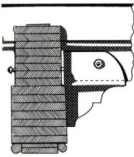

tecture; it would be more accurate to say that a generation vitally anxious to rationalize its feeling for revolutionary design grasped the doctrine as a challenging and exciting one. The *myth* of new materials, derived from historical evaluations, has had a greater effect on architecture than any technological change in itself. 6

However, advances in technology have had more to do with architectural design than providing new materials. Both steel and reinforced concrete are designed by highly abstract analytical methods that determine their configuration. Mechanical and electrical systems are also abstract in their impact on a building. Although the material manifestation is determined by these and other systems, the cause and effect is not nearly as direct as in classical construction. Forms and shapes are determined by industrial processes as much as by immediate site or functional concerns. The result for modern form is an abstract, nontactile experience primarily spatial rather than material.

ORGANIZATION

Another aspect of Cartesian geometry is its grid, a system of coordinates based on equal increments measured in three dimensions. The regularization of measurement was carried to its ultimate development in the metric system adopted in France in 1799. This is a completely rationalized system of interrelated measurements that has gradually become standard for most of the developed countries outside of the United States. Linear measurements are no longer related to parts of the body, such as the inch or the foot, but to the wave length of light, considered a constant.

Easily comprehensible measurements enable rationalized construction and the manufacture of standard parts. Beaux-Arts designs were commonly based on an abstract planning grid, a practice developed further in modern design. The seamless, undifferentiated space that was the ideal of Miës van der Rohe responds to a modern understanding of economics as the need for flexibility in planning. Miës's architecture became a standard for office buildings in the twentieth century.

Streets and Site Planning

At the juncture of the states of Utah, Colorado, Arizona, and New Mexico, there is a marker for the 90-degree intersection. A road map of North and South Dakota will reveal a rectilinear grid of highways with towns located at the junctions. Detroit was laid out with a series of straight roads at one-mile increments from the center. New York and San Francisco are examples of major cities developed by an incremental grid.

Most modern cities—and the modern parts of older cities—reflect the commercial development and ownership of land in their layouts. Washington, D.C., originally planned and developed to reflect the principles of modern democracy, was located as a political compromise between the northern and southern states in a relatively inhospitable site. Its street system is based on two important design elements: a Baroque system of diagonal avenues focused on the Capitol and an underlying rectangular grid. Here, at the beginning of the nineteenth century, two essentially different systems of planning were blended to generate the city that, more than any other, would represent the ideals of democracy.

More typically, a less conscious collision of commercial and technological forces shaped other cities in North America. The development of large-scale transportation ventures such as steamship terminals and railroad stations affected the organization of New York and Chicago. These technological and economic developments brought about an increase in the scale of commerce. The developing mass marketplace proved so powerful in its visual effect that zoning codes began to be

95

TECHNOLOGY:
ABSTRACTION
OF
KNOWLEDGE

Figure 49. Embarcadero, San Francisco.

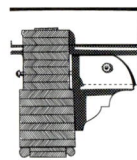

96

97

TECHNOLOGY:
ABSTRACTION
OF
KNOWLEDGE

Figure 50. Development near Ventura, California.

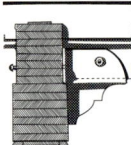

implemented. The quality of life in a modern city is mostly determined by the interaction of great, independent forces that are only faintly comprehensible.

Urban Services

The growth of engineering and technical knowledge made possible the provision of public services on a municipal scale. Traffic control systems, electric lighting, sewage disposal, water supply, and public transportation have all changed the way buildings are used. Except in cases of catastrophe, the great cycles of nature only appear to have little impact on daily life in a city. Nature is now something to be cultivated, protected, and controlled. It has been reduced to one more civic service, reflected in the greenbelts and parks designed by professional landscape architects and civil engineers.

The modern building is set against an abstract background of interacting forces, each of which can be understood and manipulated. It is their collision that is unpredictable, and those who inhabit the modern world stand at an intersection of unrelated systems.

Orientation

It is clear from the plan of Washington, D.C., that the relationship of individual blocks to the street and that of the main governmental structures is radically different. The frontal approach required by classical structures contrasts with the diagonal, dynamic view of a block front seen in passing.

The frontality of classical buildings is hierarchical. It is meant to emphasize what is considered important. When related to a compass orientation, it most often has to do with capturing light and shade on the central façade, except in the case of churches, which traditionally face east.

In contrast, the exterior of modern buildings is determined by a series of functional and economic decisions. The availability of modern glazing materials allows a great degree of control over the transparency of a wall, and the determinants of view, of privacy, and of climate control are usually in conflict. Economics dictate a similarity of treatment of the sides other than the front. Where budgets allow, the entire configuration of the building may be shaped by environmental forces as at Le Corbusier's *Unité d'Habitation* at Marseilles or any of Wright's later houses. One of the major developments of Wright's work between the Prairie and the Usonian periods was his changing attitude toward frontality. The Prairie houses retained a classical ideal of social hierarchy that disappeared entirely in the Usonians.

MODULE

Modularity was certainly not invented in the modern era, but its nature changed between the nineteenth and twentieth centuries. In classical buildings, the module was structural, derived from the span permitted in stone or wooden beams. In two dimensions, this refers to the span between columns. In three dimensions it is the structure of a square or rectilinear cell, either domed, groin-vaulted, or with a flat, paneled ceiling. The module expresses a relationship between smaller and greater spaces, as in the side aisles and chapels of classical churches. Important rooms in palaces would not typically be expressed as multiples of a structural module, but as a single bay of a larger module, possibly through the use of a giant order. By the time that iron and steel were introduced, the classical system was approaching crisis, stretched by the new materials to proportions that were decidedly not classical. The main palace at Versailles is a notable example.

Modern design depends on standards developed by professional experts. The structural bay is still a significant

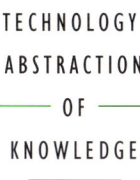

Figure 51. Entrance, University Library, Otaniemi, Finland. Alvar Aalto, 1970.

modular element, but the curtain wall, the air-tempering system, and building codes all provide minimal or optimal measurements for different elements. It is typical of modern office buildings to include columns within spaces, expressing the module directly as a multiple of the bay rather than emphasizing a contrast between large spaces with clear spans and the smaller bay of the typical module.

The Building Unit

The construction bay is handled somewhat differently by the two modern construction systems, steel and reinforced concrete. The size of the structural steel bay is typically about 30 feet by 30 feet with a floor height of 12 or 13 feet. This provides regular open space suitable for general office use. Interior columns are usually expressed to some degree, and modifications of the bay depend on local site conditions rather than use.

Reinforced concrete, on the other hand, offers more flexibility in the shape of columns and is more likely to be modified to match a functional unit, as is typical in apartment buildings. In such cases, free-standing interior columns are rarely obvious, and the building and functional unit can be said to be the same. Le Corbusier's prototype *Unité d' habitation* was configured this way.

Chapter 3

CULTURE: A CHANGE OF SCALE

When the scope of knowledge becomes so vast that no single individual, however well-educated, can comprehend any single part of it, a cultural fragmentation results which may be seen as a change of the scale of civilization itself. One way of describing the great changes brought about by the growth of democracy, coupled with the enormous impact of industrial technology, is to say that the circulation of ideas has reversed itself from top-down to bottom-up. The academies and learned societies of the eighteenth century were closely connected with the central government and survived through patronage. The advance of scientific knowledge was channeled into areas that interested the propertied class. Little concern was given to the rest of the population. In reaction to the academies, *avant-garde* movements in all of the arts were active by the late 1800s. They specifically challenged the proprieties, privileges, and courtesies of their respective professions and sought a basis for artistic expression outside of the control of the propertied classes. An interest in the daily life of ordinary people was a thread common among these movements. In literature, Proust celebrated the trivial incidents of daily life in *A la recherche du temps perdu*. Joyce based his *Ulysses* on a single day of no particular importance in the life of an ordinary man.

In the nineteenth century, independent universities and colleges were founded in the United States, Canada, Brazil, and Argentina. These institutions were mutually competitive and provided an expanded seedbed for new ideas. Every citizen had access to them, and the locus of culture was dispersed, distributed more generally than when it was centered on the capital city or town.

With the dissolution of the family-based social structure, the cult of taste grew to a new importance. An oligarchy of the arts replaced royal patronage:

> [The Elizabethan] style of ornamentation was done away with by Inigo Jones and his successors, who restored the architectural character of the ceiling, whether flat or vaulted; and thereafter paneling persisted in England until the French Revolution brought about the general downfall of taste.   1

Approaching a Definition of Modernism

The nature of modernism—what it is and where it comes from—has been the single overriding issue for esthetics in the twentieth century. Modernism is more than a style. It is a mode of contemporary life. It includes what must be excluded by the classical ideal: the uncertain, the unique, and the individual.

Proportion in Classicism

The essence of classical styles is *proportion*, the relation of parts to a whole. The discourse that occurs in a great example of classical architecture tells of how individual elements can be accommodated in a hierarchical organization. This accommodation can be more or less comfortable, as comparisons between Bramante and Michelangelo, for example, or between Bernini and Borromini have demonstrated.

Autocratic governments have found classical styles amenable to their needs. Classical grandeur persuades the individual that safety lies in accepting one's position in supporting the order of the day. Within individual expressions of the classical order, as found in houses or even furniture and decorative objects, lies the theme of pride in one's place in society.

> There are two ways of being in scale: there is the scale of proportion, and what might be called the scale of appropriateness. The former is a matter of actual measurement, while the latter is regulated solely by the nicer standard of good taste.   2

With the rise of democratic governments late in the eighteenth century, a different interpretation of classical architecture was sought. The search coincided approximately with important archeological discoveries in Greece and Italy. It was considered suitable for the new institutions of democratic government in France and the United States to be housed in structures that resembled the monuments of the birthplace of democracy, Greece in the fifth century B.C. The resulting revivalism of Greek and Italianate styles of an archaeologically correct nature brought about a dialectic in the development of architectural form that eventually resulted in the birth of modernism parallel to the revivalist forms of correct classicism. Frank Lloyd Wright described the former thus:

> Nature furnished the materials for architectural motifs out of which the architectural forms as we know them to-day have been developed, and, although our practice for centuries has been for the most part to turn from her, seeking inspiration in books and adhering slavishly to dead formulae, her wealth of suggestion is inexhaustible; her riches greater than any man's desire. I know with what suspicion the man is regarded who refers matters of fine art back to Nature. I know that it is usually an ill-advised return that is attempted, for Nature in external, obvious aspect is the usually accepted sense of the term and the nature that is reached. But given inherent vision there is no source so fertile, so suggestive, so helpful esthetically for the architect as a comprehension of natural law. As Nature is never right for a picture so is she never right for the architect—that is, not ready-made. Nevertheless, she has a practical school beneath her more obvious forms in which a sense of proportion may be cultivated, when Vignola and Vitruvius fail as they must always fail.   3

Both Edith Wharton and Frank Lloyd Wright are referring to the mathematical basis of natural forms when they speak of proportion. Wharton supposes that the ultimate manifestation of accord between architecture and nature was achieved in the classicism of the Renaissance, based on Roman models. Wright seeks confirmation of his esthetic devices from direct observation of natural models.

Where these approaches diverged was in the development of advanced science. In D'Arcy Thompson's *On Growth and Form* can be found a natural world based not on static perfection but on force and movement:

> In the Newtonian language of elementary physics, force is recognized by its action in producing or in changing motion, or in preventing change of motion or in maintaining rest. When we deal with matter in the concrete, force does not, strictly speaking, enter into the question, for force, unlike matter, has no independent objective existence. It is energy in its various forms, known or unknown, that acts upon matter. But when we abstract our thoughts from the material to its form, or from the thing moved to its motions, when we deal with the subjective conceptions of form, or movement, or the movements that change of form implies, then Force is the appropriate term for our conception of the causes by which these Forms and changes of form are brought about. When we use the term force, we use it, as the physicist always does, for the sake of brevity, as in a symbol for the magnitude and direction of an action in reference to the symbol or diagram of a material thing. It is a term as subjective and symbolic as form itself, and so is used appropriately in connection therewith.
>
> The form, then, of any portion of matter, whether it be living or dead, and the changes of form which are apparent in its movement and in its growth, may in all cases alike be described as due to the action of force. In short, the form of an object is a "diagram of forces", in this sense, at least, that from it we can judge of or deduce the forces that are acting or have acted upon it: in this strict and particular sense, it is a diagram—in the case of a solid, of the forces which *have* been impressed upon it when its conformation was produced, together with those which enable it to retain its conformation in the case of a liquid (or of a gas) of the forces which are for the moment acting on it to restrain or balance its own inherent mobility. In an organism, great or small, it is not merely the nature of the *motions* of the living substance which we must interpret in terms of force (according to kinetics), but also the conformation of the organism itself, whose permanence or equilibrium is explained by the interaction or balance of forces, as described in statics.
>
> If we look at the living cell of an Amoeba or a Spirogyra, we see a something which exhibits certain active movements, and a certain fluctuating, or more or less lasting, form; and its form at a given moment, just like its motions, is to be investigated by the help of physical methods, and explained by the invocation of the mathematical conception of force.
>
> Now the state, including the shape or form, of a portion of matter is the resultant of a number of forces, which represent or symbolise the manifestations of various kinds of energy; and it is obvious, accordingly, that a great part of physical science must be understood or taken for granted as the necessary preliminary to the discussion in which we are engaged. 4

The statement above has been quoted at length because it contains several points that are crucial for the conception of modernism in art and architecture. These points may be summarized as follows:

1. *Force . . . has no independent objective existence.* In fact, Albert Einstein and other physicists were in the process of showing that force, or energy, is equivalent to matter, an idea that would enhance this view of modern art.

2. *When we deal with the subjective conceptions of form, . . . then Force is the appropriate term for our conception of the causes by which these Forms and changes of form are brought about.* Physical form is to be regarded as the result of action.

3. *In short, the form of an object is a "diagram of forces."* Material form is to resemble an abstraction of balanced motion.

4. *Form at a given moment . . . is to be investigated by the help of physical methods, and explained by the invoca-*

tion of the mathematical conception of force. Understanding of material form is derived from a sophisticated intellectual analysis of the forces acting on it, rather than by direct, tectonic experience.

5. *The shape or form ... of a portion of matter is the resultant of a number of forces.* Material form is irreducibly complex.

Thus, proportion is not a timeless ratio of smaller to larger, but a relationship between a material result and the action of forces that have produced it.

Hierarchy in Classicism

Classicism has always been *hierarchical* in nature. It is based on a belief in a single supreme order of clear relative values that can be reflected in a closed, complete structure with all parts and subsystems articulated according to an organizing principle. Whether it is the egalitarian classicism of equal bays typical of the early Renaissance or the Imperial classicism of Palladio, Michelangelo, and the Baroque, classicism is about answers, not questions. It excludes the unknown as well as the unknowable and the uncertain. It is always the style of choice for the powerful, the vested, and the conservative.

> In deciding upon a scheme of decoration, it is necessary to keep in mind the relation of furniture to ornament, and of the room as a whole to other rooms in the house.... Every house should be decorated according to a carefully graduated scale of ornamentation culminating in the most important room of the house; but this plan must be carried out with such due sense of the relation of the rooms to each other that there shall be no violent break in the continuity of treatment. 5

Modernism is a way of understanding the world as a dynamic action. It follows from the discoveries of contemporary science as well as the development of democracies on a large scale. It marks a major stage in the growth of human understanding, leading as well as following the developments of the general culture. Modernism includes what has come before it, but is also distinct from that.

When a culture begins to deal seriously with the uncertain, the unique, and the individual, revolts against classicist hierarchies erupt. Modernism acknowledges the exigencies and circumstances of particular places and locations. It derives meaning from the particularities of client, program, and construction technology. Classicism, on the other hand, seeks to integrate the particular into a harmonious generality. Thus, for example, the Bank of England and Penn Station were based on the Hellenic Doric order, whereas the Federal Reserve Bank in New York is a Tuscan palazzo. The details of function and expression of purpose are irrelevant in the City Beautiful.

> Some lofty comments, like space and number, involve truths remote from the category of causation; and here we must be content, as Aristotle says, if the mere facts be known. But natural history deals with ephemeral and accidental, not eternal nor universal things; their causes and effects thrust themselves on our curiosity, and become the ultimate relations to which our contemplation extends. 6

When the foundations of certainty are undermined, as they certainly have been in the developed world, art begins to explore further. When the body of common knowledge grows so large that no single person, no modern Leonardo, can possibly comprehend even a small significant part of it, an architecture of uncertainty develops.

> The social history of our times seems to be moving simultaneously in two opposite directions. On the one hand there is a drastic flattening out of society, a reduction to

uniformity in opportunity and reward based on an old conception of social justice which is only now beginning to beget its full realization. On the other hand, there is the enhanced evaluation of the individual and his life and it is in this direction that we must look for the fruitful development of modern architecture. 7

It is therefore pertinent to explore exactly what modernism means in a cultural sense, and what its defining characteristics are in architecture.

Cultural Development

The culture of the United States has always been most strongly and individually expressed through its architecture. This has come about because of the intense building activity needed to fill half a continent with the cities, towns, and settlements of a new society. But it is also striking that one of the founders of American democracy, Thomas Jefferson, was himself an architect of the most didactic sort. Thus, the question of architectural style has always had a political context in the United States, and Jefferson's legacy can still be seen, for example, in the thousands of "colonial" porticos that shelter the drive-in windows of thousands of local banks in the suburbs of the eastern states.

The growth of the new American republic in the nineteenth century was accompanied by a great increase in religious free-thinking and philosophical speculation. It is quite startling in the supposedly liberated twentieth century to learn about the flexibility and tolerance present in much of the nation a hundred and fifty years ago. It was a time for founding new institutions, of questioning and experimentation, that seems very distant from today.

The great architect Henry Hobson Richardson is important to this discussion for several reasons. He was a prosperous and prolific practitioner at a time of social and economic change. He developed a cohesive style that, although revivalist in derivation, was in large part formed from a denial of classical imperatives and that exhibits many of the components of the developing modern style, as described earlier.

In a certain sense, of course, Richardson was very much a player in the Revivalist atmosphere of his time. One cannot deny his obviously Romanesque sources. But there is also a flavor of the Baroque in Henry Hobson Richardson. The undulations of seventeenth century Italian architects such as Borromini can be compared to the subtle articulation of Sever Hall at Harvard University, as well as to much of Richardson's work. Common to both was the expression of interior space as a positive force shaping the exterior façade. This characteristic of the space having a substance of its own in contradiction to its enclosure would turn out to be a key device in the emerging modern styles. In his late works, Richardson's design became quite abstract and very prophetic of things to come.

Richardson's style is the last that was successfully incorporated into the whole range of public and private building types in America. A profound change in the culture of the United States began in the late 1880s that can best be discerned in the Columbian Exhibition of 1893 in Chicago. There a strongly conservative note was struck in the planning of the exhibition and its buildings by Daniel Burnham and other commercial architects. It reemphasized the prime importance of classical tradition for architecture and proposed that the future be linked to this tradition. The dissenting vote was cast by Louis Sullivan in his Transportation Building, which was at the same time *retardataire* in detailing and advanced in its expression of contemporary construction techniques. What is most significant about the 1893 exposition for this study is that it established a hold on revivalist invention that limited its range to the classical.

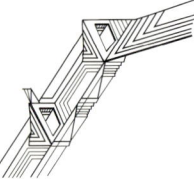

Figure 52. Oratorio of S. Filippo Neri, Rome. Francesco Borromini, 1637.

Other styles, such as the Gothic of Maybeck or the adobe of Irving Gill, would shed decorative devices that recalled the past in favor of modernist abstraction.

The late nineteenth century was marked both by the concentration of great wealth in the United States through financial vehicles such as the corporation and by the opening of the formerly isolationist culture to other influences. These include the cultures of Africa, through the large population of newly freed slaves, of Native America, and of Asia, specifically Japan. The emergence of the classical revival at this time is a sign of the retrenchment of the conservative culture against such foreign influences.

In 1893, the 25-year-old Frank Lloyd Wright, who had just been fired from the practice of Louis Sullivan and was newly set up on his own, saw the Japanese exhibition at the Columbian Exposition. His incorporation of Japanese principles of design into his work inevitably set him apart from the mainstream and would shut him out of consideration for major projects until the 1930s, when a conservative version of the modern style, called the International Style, would at last make itself (and, by association, Wright himself) acceptable to commercial interests.

Meanwhile, the conservative element that dominated the Exhibition had strengthened its hold on American architecture. The City Beautiful movement, exemplified in works by Daniel Burnham and McKim, Mead & White, made its powerful assertion of classicism in Utopian form at a time of great economic opportunity and civic development. This movement is connected with Europe through the Ecole des Beaux-Arts and the Haussmann plan for Paris and can itself be interpreted as an "International Style." The effect of City Beautiful development intensified the disjuncture between contemporary reality and the classical vision of the future, a disjuncture that can be seen, ironically, as a rich source for the growth of the modern vision, incorporated in a critical sense.

Against the retreat of mainstream American culture into its classical shell must be placed the explosion of knowledge in the sciences around the turn of the century. Questions raised by the studies of Einstein in physics and Freud in psychology only hastened the fragmentation of culture in their threat to the hegemony of the conservative core. In the novels of Wharton and James we read of wealthy Americans newly sensitive to issues of class and besieged by the claims of an increasingly modern world. In art, the primitivist visions of Picasso, Matisse, and Gauguin were rejected in favor of the more comforting images of Whistler and Renoir. In music, Stravinsky and Schoenberg presaged a profound split that would occur between the conservative classical form, popular with audiences increasingly unwilling to listen to twentieth century compositions, and the "popular" form of jazz, primarily a creation of African Americans. For the first two decades of the twentieth century, in New York as well as other North American cities, the City Beautiful held sway.

In fact, the self-distinguishing tendency of private capital conflicted with the Haussmann-Burnham vision of uniformity, and the classically detailed jumble of façades along Broadway in lower Manhattan is testimony to the problems of applying the City Beautiful to the city actual. At the American Telephone & Telegraph Building in lower Manhattan, correctly proportioned colonnades were stacked like six-packs in a convenience store. When this building was renovated after AT&T's departure to even more bizarre quarters uptown during the 1980s, a particularly striking glass tower was added to its west end, providing a convincing answer to the question of classical proportion in a modern world.

CULTURE: A CHANGE OF SCALE

Figure 53. Commercial buildings on lower Broadway, Manhattan.

109

CULTURE:
A CHANGE
OF
SCALE

Figure 54. American Telephone & Telegraph Company Building, lower Manhattan. Welles Bosworth, 1915–22.

110

Figure 55. Hotel Macklowe, lower Manhattan. Eli Attia, 1991.

Although Wright had locked himself into the progressive minority by his acceptance of Japanese and, later, Native American influences, Le Corbusier—involved with radical art movements that were themselves strongly influenced by the designs of African art—fared little better in gaining influence until the 1920s, when, faced with the devastation of World War I, continental European societies began to tolerate, at least in intellectual circles, socially progressive ideas and forms of culture. When it was conclusively demonstrated at the Weissenhof Exhibition of housing in Stuttgart in 1927 that the new style could be built for a significantly lower cost than the reigning classical with its heavy ornament and articulation, the stage was set for a change.

In New York, the economic advantages of a flexibly modern style had already been noticed. The corporate architect Ralph Walker designed a series of commercial skyscrapers, primarily for the Bell Telephone Company, that successfully incorporated the modern concept of disjuncture. The New York Telephone Company Building generates a symmetrical façade by slicing the corners of its tower along the Sixth Avenue diagonal. The intersecting masses are clearly indicated, while the detailing of the brick transforms it into a voluptuously plastic screen worthy of Borromini. This is carried further in the limestone and marble Irving Trust Headquarters, where decorative incisions pass unaffected across joints between materials in a sophisticated, modern manner.

The decisive event in the acceptance of a conservative form of modernism in America was the show of 1930 at the Museum of Modern Art on the International Style. Although Le Corbusier was lionized as the most significant modern architect, his production would be channeled to progressive housing complexes in the suburbs, city plans that were largely unrealized, and institutional buildings in foreign countries. By his own determination, through publishing his designs and public speeches, to present his view, he had an enormous influence on architecture later in the century. But it was Ludwig Miës van der Rohe who reaped most of the reward for accommodating radical modernist ideas to the conservative tastes of commercial America.

As proposed elsewhere in this study, the codification of the Modern Movement in the garb of the International Style focused serious attention on that movement at the expense of others, certainly just as vital and perhaps more so in the context of the United States than in Europe. Most striking is the case of Frank Lloyd Wright, whose truly revolutionary style can be seen even today as far ahead of most contemporary trends.

The other side of this coin is the acceptance of work essentially classical in configuration but built in the materials of the Modern Movement. The result, as at Lincoln Center, was a reclothing of classicism in the garb of the progressives. The question that inevitably comes up is of the difference between a steel-framed building with a full complement of twentieth century services arrayed with classically correct colonnades and a similar structure sporting a curtain wall. Miës's work at the Seagram Building reveals how modernism incorporates classical principles while denying their hegemony over the whole.

The comparison of Miës's post office in Chicago with McKim, Mead & White's New York post office of 1912 revealed an identity of formal approach that questioned the modern content of the former. Apart from the modern quality of transparency, the absence of disjuncture is symptomatic, revealing a conservative classicism that casts light on the purported "failure" of modernism, a critical view prevalent in the 1970s.

III

CULTURE:
A CHANGE
OF
SCALE

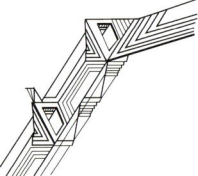

Figure 56. New York Telephone Company Building, lower Manhattan. Voorhees, Gmelin & Walker, 1932.

113

CULTURE:
A CHANGE
OF
SCALE

Figure 57. Irving Trust Company headquarters, lower Manhattan. Voorhees, Gmelin & Walker, 1932.

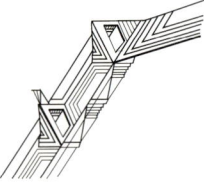

Many architects and critics have addressed this issue, left unresolved by the International Style. Contemporary practitioners in the classical style argue that classicism is a way of seeing and ordering the world and maintaining continuity with the culture of western Europe that is at least twenty-five hundred years old. They point out that essential human functions and actions have not changed and are, in fact, universal. The classical style, they claim, has been developed over a much longer time than any other and possesses unsurpassed richness and sophistication.

The appalling results of classical half-truths applied in the garb of "post-modernism" is evidence enough of the difficulties for contemporary classicism. The development of modern styles in the United States, at least, derives from the inevitable transformation of American culture from the unilateral, Europeanized classicism of the City Beautiful to an indeterminable, ever-changing consensus of many different approaches. Disjuncture as a characteristic of modern form, then, gains its significance from its relevance to a multicultural society and, indeed, a multicultural world.

SPACE

The importance of the modern notion of space as a dynamic, positive element in design cannot be overestimated. This is not to say that classical architecture and painting had not dealt with the spatial qualities of buildings. Christian Norberg-Schulz, among others, has written extensively about the dynamic spatial qualities of Late Baroque and Rococo buildings.[8] His excellent analyses of Bohemian Baroque churches such as the one at Vierzehnheiligen describes how the classical structural system seems to be warped by the pressure of elliptical spatial cells.

However, this is a modern interpretation from a critic noted for his sensitivity to modernism. The response of classical systems to notions of the growing independence of space is a symptom of the developing modern world, where space itself would become the supreme concept for architecture. The interaction of independent spatial and structural systems is one of the primary characteristics of modern buildings.

> The distinguishing aesthetic principles of the International Style as laid down by the authors are three: emphasis upon volume—space enclosed by thin planes or surfaces as opposed to the suggestion of mass and solidity; regularity as opposed to symmetry or other kinds of obvious balance; and, lastly, dependence upon the intrinsic elegance of materials, technical perfection, and fine proportions, as opposed to applied ornament. [9]

Closely connected with the modern idea of space is the loss of what can best be termed spirituality. The great unifying idea of Renaissance art was humanism, a focus on the perception of an individual human being. It is this idea that would inevitably develop into the modern political theory of democracy. But for a long time, humanist art asserted the identity of mankind with the divine. Painting and literature depicted heaven and hell and their connection with ordinary lives. Architecture, too, through the classical system, represented an element of the divine on earth. When one experienced the great rooms of a palace or the crossing of a church, a specific representation of an ethereal world was understood.

In the modern era, this representational quality was completely transformed to a much more abstract understanding of space itself. There was no longer any such thing as holy ground, and the imagination could no longer rely on traditional images of religious concepts. Instead, a more scientific or technical view of the world took the place of religious conviction. Where the classical system evoked an ordered world based on divine harmony, the modern eye sees how something was made. It understands the classical connection but does not experience it. The relationship of humankind to the universe has been transformed.

For the world appears different to modern eyes. The great ideas in painting, literature, and music that sprang up around the turn of the twentieth century broke the hegemony of classicism on the individual's view of the world, replacing it with concepts derived from the process of creating art. Thus, the Impressionist and Cubist painters abstracted light, color, and form from what they saw and rendered subject matter irrelevant. Symbolist authors explored what they believed to be the unconscious mind—a new idea in itself—rather than the morals and values of human relationships. The structure of the novel changed from the terraced action and balanced morality of Thomas Hardy to the evenly paced work of Joyce. The symphony, having finally achieved a perfected sonata-allegro form, was no longer of prime interest for the brightest musicians, who tried to break free of the key-centered classical structure.

Similarly in architecture, the representation of legitimate authority that is the essence of the classical system—hence its perennial popularity with those in power—becomes a denial of authority for the modern architect, who proposes, in its place, an identification with the user as well as the owner. This equivalence of conflicting influences is the primary subject matter of modernism.

Enclosure

In a democracy, one's status is provisional. Life is experienced as a series of changing options that must be adapted to fit one's sense of self. The fracture of identity that results from living in a democratic society affects how buildings and spaces are perceived. As the mind expands beyond the limits of the body, space reaches out beyond walls.

The wall itself, then, becomes ambiguous. The famous *collages* of Miës van der Rohe show virtual surfaces defining spaces in a minimal way, themselves no more than two-dimensional planes of reference that are completely changeable. Space is independent of these planes to a great degree. It can flow unimpeded to encompass areas of activity that are both indoor and outdoor. Space is to modernism what gravity was to classicism.

At Morse and Stiles Colleges, designed for Yale University in 1958 by Eero Saarinen, the walls are constructed of large rocks and boulders held in a matrix of concrete formed by geometrically flat surfaces and partially washed away to reveal the stones. The denial of the weight and structural possibilities of the stones turns them into massive decoration and ironically lightens the walls as enclosure. This treatment is in direct contrast to the massive, Gothic Revival gymnasium, completed only thirty years previously, and visible between the colleges.

Privacy

The examination of the family, through the professionalization of sociology and psychology, challenged tradition and changed the nature of privacy. The achievement—or maintaining—of status that was formerly the thrust of family life became secondary to one's individual sense of happiness. The novels of Henry James and Edith Wharton are full of conflicts between propriety and sensibility, indicating the great change that was taking place.

From the classical palace, with its carefully separated public and private zones and its hierarchical arrangement of rooms, the modern house began to shake itself free. Func-

116

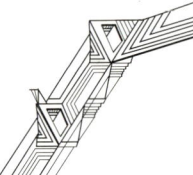

Figure 58. Morse and Stiles Colleges, Yale University. Eero Saarinen, 1958–62.

tional concerns such as considerations of light and view and accommodation of specific activities replaced the representation of status.

Shelter

In rejecting the classical hierarchy, modern architects looked to primitive sources of shelter and to other civilizations. The interest in shelter, where nature responds to the individual in a personal way, is quite distinct from the classical ideal of the house for a god. The foreign sources that influenced American and European art during the nineteenth and early twentieth centuries included civilizations as rigid and structured as that of eighteenth century Europe: Japan, China, pre-Columbian Mexico, the Ottoman Empire, Persia. What proved influential, however, was the properties that could be abstracted from these sources, again breaking their hegemony. It was the regularity of the Japanese structural system and particularly the modular *tatami* mat that was chosen by such architects as Frank Lloyd Wright to create the new modernism.

There was always ambivalence in the early modern work. In specifically denying the classical system, modern architecture in a sense included it as one aspect of a dialogue about the importance of modern living. The dialogue was clear for as long as classicism itself could be an important source of design ideas. It was later in the modern era, after the triumph of the International Style, that modernism's reactive side became problematic. The Pan-Pacific Auditorium in Los Angeles is an example of work that denies classical decoration and proportion while retaining symmetry and axiality. Although the importance of surface differences is not negligible, the tactility and materiality of classically derived systems remains attractive.

Outside and Inside

At the palace of Versailles, the bedroom of the king represented the center of the universe. The closer one was to that room, the higher one's position in the society of the time. The plan and gardens of Versailles emphasize this hierarchy through their configuration as a series of stages along an axial path focused on the king. To be included in the patronage of the court, one had to accept the style in fashion.

> To conform to a style, then, is to accept those rules of proportion which the artistic experience of centuries has established as the best, while within those limits allowing free scope to the individual requirements which must inevitably modify every house or room adapted to the use and convenience of its occupants.
>
> There is one thing more to be said in defence of conformity to style; and that is, the difficulty of getting rid of style. Strive as we may for originality, we are hampered at every turn by an artistic tradition of over two thousand years....
>
> The styles especially suited to modern life have already been roughly indicated as those prevailing in Italy since 1500, in France from the time of Louis XIV, and in England since the introduction of the Italian manner by Inigo Jones.... 10

With modern architecture, the emphasis changed from orientation toward a symbolic location to multiple visual and circulation axes inherent in the site and functional program. The distinction between inside and outside is merely physical and without cosmic significance. This change is most notable in modern places of worship, which, to be successful, must dramatize the act of approach and the views or lighting in some way, as in Le Corbusier's churches at La Tourette and Ronchamp and Wright's Beth Sholom Synagogue in Philadelphia. Otherwise, contemporary churches are singu-

118

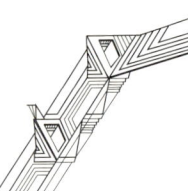

Figure 59. Pan-Pacific Auditorium, Los Angeles. Wurdeman & Becket, 1935.

119

CULTURE:
A CHANGE
OF
SCALE

larly lacking in the spiritual quality of, for example, the Renaissance churches of Florence. The sacredness of a place is not a concept that suits modern styles. Congregational churches and Quaker meeting houses, bathed in the lucidity of daylight, are the prototypes of modernism.

Exclusion and Inclusion

Classical art had a whole range of approved subjects, including Bible stories, myths, and moral lessons. These were to be represented by the artist in a manner that enhanced their meaning. In modern times, the subject matter of art directs itself to the commonplace. The representational characteristic of classicism was dropped in modern art. The subject of art became the process of its own creation, including the perceptions of the artist, the recording of events, and the interaction of the materials when formed into the piece. In architecture, as the representation of Greek temples and Renaissance palaces was repudiated, the expression of modern systems came to dominate: spatial, functional, structural, and mechanical. It is thus not surprising that the classical architects favored today tend to be those, such as Borromini and Vanbrugh, who challenged in some way the classical system and were not considered as important in their own time as they are now.

With the open-ended subject matter of modern architecture comes the constant reevaluation of priorities and conflicts between design elements. The exclusion of ornament per se represents the denial of traditional values against the presence of material reality.

Ownership

Citizenship was vested in the landowner in classical societies, along with education, social acceptance, and the other privileges of social status. The compartmentation of spaces in classical palaces reflected the strictness of the hierarchical order and emphasized separation. The modern concept of space is of a continuous flow across boundaries, with overlapping of functions and multiple definitions of the same area. It emphasizes continuity, expressing the fluidity of social change.

The divorce of ownership and occupancy produces an unresolvable conflict in the modern world. The sources of capital that support the construction of modern buildings have become more and more separated from their users, whose physical and functional requirements must be met. The spatial manifestation of this conflict can be seen in the separation of screen-walls and structure so common in the work of the great modernists.

GEOMETRY

One aspect of the classical system was its basis in mathematics. Simple numeric ratios were considered important in the generation of building plans, and Palladio's drawings are annotated with the relative lengths of walls and elevations in his *I Quattro Libri*. The goal of classical mathematics was to develop a completely closed, self-proving system that could quantify all the elements and processes of the universe.

Ultimately, mathematicians began reaching into areas that were problematic for the classical ideal. Imaginary numbers, real and unreal numbers, and the quantification of the unknowable were all blows to the heart for classical hegemony. By the time of the theories of Einstein at the beginning of the twentieth century, mathematics had modernized itself beyond the immediately comprehensible.

One result of the quantification of classical design was the idea of proportion. Mathematically a comparison of two unlike quantities, proportion could be used to justify a natural difference in the status of individuals. If one were well-born, one would have senses that could better perceive the subtleties of proportion. Whether or not one could be educated to improve one's perception was an issue for debate, since the belief in the universal good of learning is much more recent than the belief in natural differences between races and social status.

The Golden Mean is a ratio such that the relationship between the two numbers is equal to that between the larger number and the sum of the two. It calculates as an irrational number, one that cannot be reduced to a simple, whole-number ratio. In classical theory, it could generate a rectangle of particularly pleasing proportion.

> To the fastidious eye [the charm of a room] will, of course, be found in fitness of proportion, in the proper use of each moulding and in the harmony of all the decorative processes; and even to those who think themselves indifferent to such detail, much of the sense of restfulness and comfort produced by certain rooms depends on the due adjustment of their fundamental parts. 11

Although the idea was accepted by no less than Le Corbusier as the basis for *le Modulor*, his planning module for his later work, there is no evidence that such a proportion is perceptible in any precise way in three-dimensional space.

The most common application of the rules of proportion in classical theory is to establish a ratio of part to whole, or of side to side, that will then be used as much as possible to determine all of the measurements of the building. Palladio's work reflects this theory in applying simple, whole-number ratios to plans and elevations. That the Golden Mean is not a simple, whole-number ratio identifies an unresolved conflict in proportional theory. One person's simplicity is another's complexity.

Cartesian Solids

Around the turn of the eighteenth century, the reappraisal of simple geometric shapes undertaken by Ledoux, Boulée, and others marked an increasing degree of abstraction that would ultimately permeate the modern view of culture. It was not just the use of these shapes but their application that was distinctive. Functional applications were forced into spaces allocated for them in a way that was clearly not intended for construction.

The abstract representation of geometric solids would again become important with the development of framed building systems: steel and concrete. Factory-made building components lend themselves well to precise, flat surfaces. Coupled with the transparency of large areas of glass, it became easy to articulate building masses clearly by minimizing surface pattern and detail.

Tectonics

Classical architecture has an immediacy that has proved to be difficult to achieve for modern architects. The sense of weight and pressure, of solid mass and void that is the hallmark of good classical rendering is made possible by a simple duality of solid and void, the *poché* that is the hallmark of classical planning. The sculpted quality of classical detail reinforces one's tactile sense and engages the observer in a unique way.

This solidity would be diminished by the historical and technological forces that brought about the modern era. A skyscraper is essentially light rather than heavy. There is a dissociation for the observer between the size of the building—usually much larger in volume than a typical classical building—and how it is supported. The calculations that allow structural frames to be designed are of a higher order than those for solid masonry and cannot be readily intuited

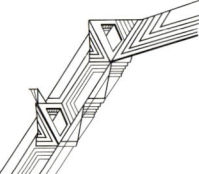

without a technical education. Although a modern monument such as the Citicorp Tower in Manhattan can provide excellent public facilities, the building itself has a deadness that is characteristic of abstract, modern buildings.

Dynamic Form

Much of the presence of classical buildings comes from their sense of inevitability and solidity. The harmony expressed by a well-proportioned classical façade implies completeness and permanence. In modern buildings, this sense of permanence has been replaced with something that is about time, rather than apart from time. This is readily apparent in the gradual development of skyscraper design from the tripartite base-shaft-capital arrangement of the early twentieth century, through the chiseled mass approach of the 1920s and 1930s to the International Style box of the 1950s and 1960s. The flatness of the top is an indication that height has become a concern not of structure but of economics: more or less stories could have been built without any significant change in the design. The generality of modern commerce has caused even custom-designed corporate headquarters buildings to seem as though they could be reoccupied by any owner.

Eero Saarinen's CBS headquarters in Manhattan displays an interesting treatment of exterior wall. In its solidity, it is classically tectonic. But the interior space is readily perceivable, and the lack of differentiation of detail from the base to the top of the stone shafts expresses the generality of modern design. Like other modern buildings, it is easily changed for different interior uses, and its mechanical systems can be updated much more readily than those in a classical building. For example, the Farley Post Office in New York—a landmarked Beaux-Arts design—had to be replaced by a new mail-handling facility in 1992 because its structural bays could no longer accommodate newer mail trucks. The connection to the adjacent railroad station, the essential functional *parti* of this post office as well as those in Philadelphia, Washington, D.C., and other cities, is no longer functionally significant.

Plasticity

The solid-void quality of classical architecture and sculpture was emphasized by the techniques of drawing and rendering taught at the Ecole des Beaux-Arts during the nineteenth century. The measurements of antique buildings made at the end of the eighteenth century at Athens, Pompeii, and Herculaneum were used to generate systems of proportion for correct detailing. Molds and profiles dictated the representation of ancient motifs that could be manufactured by the new building industries developing at the same time.

Decorative elements were gradually transferred from carving techniques to the molding and impressing typical of modern construction as solid masonry was replaced by relatively thin panels of stone, brick, or terra-cotta with prefabricated detailing. This could be charming and elegant when applied to modern building types, but the plastic quality remained only on the surface.

Advances in technical drawing supported investigations into how three-dimensional objects could be precisely described in two dimensions. Cubist painters explored the plastic possibilities of flat shapes, and new ideas about space as a dynamic medium were expressed. An interest in the layering of space developed even as new building materials themselves were coordinated into relatively thin layers.

Figure 60. Library, University of Pennsylvania. Frank Furness, 1888–1914.

CULTURE: A CHANGE OF SCALE

Virtual Space

The new idea of space meant that plasticity was visual rather than tactile. Space itself could be plastic, as in the sculpture of Calder. It was the development of space as an independent concept that inspired the early modern architects to invent a new kind of architecture. Virtual space is that which is generated by the appearance of its physical delimiters in the mind. It is divorced from the force of gravity. The modern architect suggests a space before it is occupied and then resolves the expectation with either confirmation or denial. In this manner, different spatial ideas can be generated simultaneously, leaving the observer to resolve the conflict. The engagement of the observer in this way is a hallmark of the modern approach to design. The tectonic sensation of gravity conflicts with the visual sense of space, in contrast to the classical system.

The work of the late-nineteenth-century architect Frank Furness displays his experimentation with colliding forms that begin to actualize virtual spaces. At the entrance of the Library of the University of Pennsylvania, the clarity of separation between the delicate metal handrail at the stair and the massive supporting pillar implies a penetration of the stone. The space occupied by the stair begins to achieve an independence from the entry itself, with an overlap: two comprehensible spaces occupying the same place without any attempt at subordinating one to the other.

Coordination of Systems

Symmetry is the essential classical method to achieve balance. The tripartite classical structure of beginning, middle, and end found in symphonic music, drama, and literature was applied to architecture and painting at the Beaux-Arts through the study of composition. The entire experience was to be defined and explicated through a classically ordered structural hierarchy.

In the modern era, the whole system of hierarchical control was broken down. A new dynamic idea of balance came about based on the impression of equivalent, conflicting systems. One way of achieving this was to direct circulation against the axes of a symmetrical system, as Frank Lloyd Wright did in many of his Prairie Houses. A classically balanced system perceived dynamically is essential in the modern vision. The axis created by the symmetry is not the circulation path. The experience is ambivalent, with different interpretations possible.

Polyarchy versus Hierarchy

At its core, modernism challenged the foundations of classical order, its hierarchical arrangement of parts always elucidated as to rank and position. Symmetry and centrality are paramount. Proportions are to be related and an overriding order, or proportion, is to control the whole.

> The old French and Italian architects never failed to respect that rule of decorative composition which prescribes that where there is any division of parts, one part shall unmistakably predominate.   12

In the modern view, an inclusion of alternatives, dynamically balanced so that none predominates, will generate a composite architecture. This sort of architecture, unlike the classical, is profoundly incomplete. It requires observation, an active investment by the observer to interpret and judge the experience. It is not as easy nor as comfortable as the classical experience.

Harmony

When correct proportions are applied to a classical design, a sense of harmony will be achieved in the finished building. The idea of harmony was essential to the oligarchic societies in which classicism flourished. It was claimed that all of nature supported the position of the privileged, who were as superior to the unpropertied as was their society to those considered barbarian, or as was humankind to the rest of the animal kingdom. The good of all depended on each one occupying his or her assigned place (the "hers" generally being defined according to the "his").

Understanding this aspect of the classical ideal makes the reaction to Darwin's *Origin of Species* understandable. Its publication was as shocking as any such work had ever been, for it swept away the idea of divine harmony in nature and replaced it with a dynamic model of competition and change. In cultural terms, the Western world was ready to consider such an idea and to experiment with it in all fields of endeavor, including architecture. Even art history based itself on what could be termed a Darwinian model: the evolution of styles derived from predecessors.

ORGANIZATION

The classical bay is based on the structural requirements of a masonry system, either trabeated or arcuated. The minimum support is concentrated at four corners of a rectangle, although any of the sides may be engaged for continuous support. The regularization of this system forms a grid of cells that, in the archetypal basilica plan, is configured as a large central space surrounded by ancillary cells. It is a flexible system that complements the compartmentalization of hierarchical societies.

In the modern era, the abstraction of the rectilinear grid increased. Structural concerns were no longer primary, and the cantilevering possibilities of steel and reinforced concrete frames introduced independence between the building enclosure and its structure. Circulation played more of a role in the organization of space, and separation of movement patterns was emphasized.

Streets and Site Planning

With the development of modern means of transportation, the street took on a dual character. High-speed vehicular traffic was separated from local foot traffic, and a whole series of technological changes took place to support this distinction, including drainage sewers, electric lighting, and traffic control systems. The street became related to the building in a different way. The famous Nolli plan of Rome of 1748 shows the city in terms of *poché*, the solid-void relationship that is the essence of classical materiality. Modern buildings relate to the street in a number of ways. They may lift themselves lightly above a plaza, establishing continuity between the public street and interior lobby. They may orient themselves to something other than the street, perhaps facing the sunlight instead of the building line as does Le Corbusier's *Unité d'habitation* in Marseilles. In both cases, the strong axiality of the street is opposed by a conflicting force in the design of the building. An excellent example of the complex relationship of modern buildings and streets is at Romaldo Giurgola's Penn Mutual Life Building in Philadelphia, where an existing façade was incorporated as a freestanding classical element into the design of a skyscraper.

As in much of the development of modernism, the opposition between building and street depended on the existence of classical order. Nolli's and other such plans typical of eighteenth century planning emphasize the coordination of the interiors of buildings with the street wall. Modern architecture depended for much of its impact on denying this consistency, and consciously conflicting with it, as was seen in the famous case of the Seagram Building's initial impact on the classically configured street wall of Park Avenue in Manhattan in the 1950s. Something was irrevocably lost when the older buildings were replaced by International Style office buildings of a size similar to Seagram. Morse and

CULTURE: A CHANGE OF SCALE

Figure 61. Penn Mutual Life Building, Philadelphia. Romaldo Giurgola, 1969–70.

127

CULTURE: A CHANGE OF SCALE

Figure 62. Citicorp Center, Manhattan.
Hugh Stubbins, 1975–77.

Stiles Colleges at Yale University, designed to invoke in a romantic way the charm of older streets, indicate the degree of change that had taken place by the twentieth century.

Generators of Design

Control of growing traffic among new modes of transportation was overt in the classically organized city plans of the early twentieth century. The Beaux-Arts idea sought a hierarchical consistency, referenced to classical style. This was foreshadowed at the Chicago Columbian Exposition of 1893. It could be seen again in McKim, Mead & White's plan for Washington, D.C., and in Daniel Burnham's plans for railroad stations in New York and Chicago in the early years of the twentieth century.

Railroads themselves became the generators of street plans because of the impact of their facilities on the civic infrastructure. The Crystal Palace had demonstrated the qualities of an extensive, undifferentiated interior space unlike anything in classical design, and its model was used for train sheds at major railroad stations throughout the nineteenth century. Typically, the railroad station faced the street with a classically designed block for the ticket counter, waiting room, and ancillary services while the trains themselves were approached under a steel-and-glass roof of more modern design.

This separation of classical from modern design in a single facility indicated the ambivalence of contemporary culture, just at a time when modernism was making its claim as an independent force. Grand Central Station in New York included the development of Park Avenue when it was redesigned in 1910. New buildings, most of them classically styled, were constructed above the approach tracks.

Zoning

The relationship of classical buildings to the landscape, even within a city, was simple and direct compared to the modern world. The topography of Rome can be clearly traced from Nolli's 1748 map of Rome, even considering the regularity of the streets in areas developed later. But in modern times, the emphasis was on control of the landscape. Zoning brought about commercialization of the city, where areas became more or less important based on the differential value of property. Buildings with fine finishes and public amenities would be concentrated in areas of high property value. Because this value could change, neighborhoods could rise and fall in quality over time. The city typically became a place of variable character, without the solemnity of the classical city. Washington, D.C., is one of the last classically designed cities, and it has been able to retain its character because of restrictive zoning, which restricts commercial development within the city limits. Its classical monuments set a standard for new construction that inhibits the quality of its truly modern architecture.

Axiality

The change in the nature of the axis from the classical to the modern is a change from procession to circulation. Procession is a public function, ceremonial in nature. The strict social hierarchy of eighteenth century empires supported a highly structured program of public interaction. The organization of axes and diagonals in classical planning provided a background for the parades and promenades of upper-class life. When Sixtus V planned the avenues of Rome in the sixteenth century, it was to provide direct means for pilgrims to visit the important religious monuments. Squares were marked with fountains or obelisks to reinforce the axis of movement. Similarly, Haussmann's plan for Paris developed from a need to move and support government troops in order to quell local disturbances.

But the act of imposing circulation on an existing pattern can also take a modern form. Modern planning emphasizes efficiency in the movement of crowds and the separation of inherently incompatible modes of transportation. This implies direct connections between destinations, and the coordination of conflicting circulation paths is an important element in modern design.

Campus Planning

The development of the democratic ideal in America can be traced from the planning of the first universities. The University of Virginia was intended didactically both as a model for an institution of higher learning and as an architectural prototype. The American university, as it developed, was to a certain extent a new sort of institution. It of course had connections to the great European universities, which were themselves derived from the monasteries of the Middle Ages. Many American colleges looked back to this tradition in their buildings. Yale University, in the 1920s and 1930s, mounted a substantial building campaign of notably *retardataire* structures in New Haven.

Yet there was also a movement to define a uniquely American institution. Jefferson's initial proposal at the University of Virginia for new institutions suitable for a democracy was ambivalent, modeled on existing institutions in Europe. It was only as the nation developed, particularly through the Morrill Act (1862), which gave states federal lands on which to establish colleges and the Hatch Act (1887), which extended the program, that the American system of higher education developed its own format. Thomas Jefferson's design at Virginia derives from the pedagogical impulse.

Ten residential pavilions connected by a colonnaded walkway were originally distributed symmetrically along the two sides of a rectangular court. These pavilions were detailed in variations of eighteenth century styles, adapted to the red-brick and white-wood trim typical of Colonial America. Jefferson was well aware of the Late Baroque and Classic Revival strains of contemporary French architecture and he intended the new university to represent in its architecture the stylistic alternatives for the new republic. At the high end of the court, between the two rows of pavilions, was placed a circular library derived from the Pantheon in Rome. The whole complex is developed along Palladian lines in a strict hierarchical order. But the variations in style, the differing intervals between the pavilions on each side, and certain other details display another, more experimental side to Jefferson's thinking. Among these details are the serpentine walls behind the pavilions on either side of the court. Their undulating plan enabled Jefferson to build a self-supporting wall in a single wythe of bricks without additional buttressing. But the supposed savings in material is illusory. Few, if any, additional bricks would be required to form buttresses every ten feet or so, sufficient to support the walls, and construction along a straight line would have been far easier than the curves proposed by Jefferson. Modern eyes can perhaps detect a less conscious interest: not only are the walls self-supporting, but the means by which the support is achieved is independent of the regulating principles of the rest of the complex. The rear walls are a minor element. The principles of classical architecture would dictate that they should conform in some way to the larger organizing scheme of the complex. But they may have been intentionally designed to express an independence from the overall order, to deny—even in a very minor way—the comprehensiveness of the classical colonnaded scheme.

If it can be allowed that this relatively tiny deviation from the classical order might herald the growth of modernism later in the nineteenth century, it suggests the key to a comparison between two twentieth century designs for college campuses: Wright's Florida Southern College of

130

Figure 63. Crown Hall (School of Architecture), Illinois Institute of Technology, Chicago. Ludwig Miës van der Rohe, 1950–56.

131

CULTURE:
A CHANGE
OF
SCALE

Figure 64. Corner detail, Chemistry Building, Illinois Institute of Technology, Chicago. Ludwig Miës van der Rohe, 1945.

Figure 65. House in Palm Beach, Florida. Addison Mizner, 1920–25.

133

CULTURE:
A CHANGE
OF
SCALE

1938–56 and Miës's contemporary Illinois Institute of Technology.

At Florida Southern College, Frank Lloyd Wright had the opportunity to design a new campus for an existing liberal arts college established and run by the Methodist Church. One of the most distinctive aspects of the curriculum here was a substantial program in home economics and teacher training. Loftlike open spaces similar to a factory were thus required. Residences were not part of the program.

A major difference between the American university and the European was in the nonresidential nature of the former. Even where substantial on-campus residence facilities were provided, these were almost inevitably housed in separate buildings and were administered by a separate system under a distinct nonacademic Dean. In fact, the primary impetus behind the great construction program at Yale mentioned above was to establish a residentially based college system derived from English models.

The result was that American institutions were less hierarchically organized than European universities. Although it can be maintained that the tutorial system of Oxford and Cambridge offered more individual training, the relation between tutor and student was only a single element in a strict hierarchy of professors and deans. In America, curricula were finally determined outside of the institutions by accreditation committees, either at the level of the state government or nationally. Private and public institutions were coordinated so that the system of academic credit could be applied universally. It was easy for students to transfer between institutions and even to enroll simultaneously for courses at more than one.

The architectural impact of all of this was that Wright's campus for Florida Southern emphasized the interaction of independent academic departments. There was a central auditorium/chapel, but the plan clearly shows that the circulation pattern pinwheels around this landmark rather than focusing on it.

Contemporary with Florida Southern was Ludwig Miës van der Rohe's new campus for the Illinois Institute of Technology. Here again was a vocationally oriented nonresidential campus in the American mold. Individual pavilions reflect the separation of academic departments. However, the symmetrical, axial arrangement—quite unlike that at Florida Southern College—harks back to the hierarchical organization of the traditional college. The coordination of structure and screen also derives from classical models. The plan of the campus and its associated buildings is based on a 24-square-foot grid.

The individual buildings articulate the difference between structure and screen through careful delineation of materials and details at the joints. This again is in line with classical thinking, although the materials and methods are contemporary. The use of exposed roof trusses at the department of architecture building is equivalent to the formal colonnade used to mark important parts of a structure in the classical language.

MODULE

Before the twentieth century, the attention of architects was primarily focused on buildings for the government, the church, or wealthy patrons. There was not a lot of attention given to the individual needs of ordinary people. When mass housing was considered at all, it was usually in the form of façades for blocks of buildings, with little attention to the interior. The consideration given to commerce would take the form of a covered market, as in London and Paris, or a gallery, as in Milan. In both cases, the conception was of a block subdivided to accommodate a repetitive function.

Figure 66. Inland Steel Building, Chicago. Skidmore, Owings and Merrill, 1957.

135

CULTURE:
A CHANGE
OF
SCALE

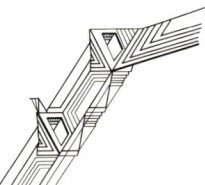

Many wealthy patrons in the contemporary world wish to achieve the status that accompanies classical and other revival styles. The houses and office buildings that result from this do not function in a substantially different way from those in the modern style, but the expression is quite different. A typical house by Addison Mizner in Palm Beach, Florida, presents the important social rooms on the Spanish-style exterior with arched windows arranged in a symmetrical hierarchy. Although not symmetrical, the major and minor axes of the house are clearly established and it achieves a presence that is substantial for a relatively informal, beachside vacation house.

In the modern mind, the planning unit took precedence, and many standards for different building types have evolved. The focus on the individual space multiplied is opposite to the classical subdivided block and generates a different sort of space. The Inland Steel headquarters is a typical International Style skyscraper from Skidmore, Owings and Merrill. Its structural lightness is clear from the degree of transparency, and the mass of the building is in balance with the individual office cells. Residential buildings of a similar size can appear in a style that makes them virtually indistinguishable from office buildings, a situation frequently derided in contemporary criticism. But classical buildings used for office or commercial functions were typically based on a *palazzo* format. The temple was originally an exalted home for a god, derived from the human residences of ancient Greece and Rome. Commercial buildings, institutions, and educational facilities and residences have all been designed as classical temples. The idea that a building should reflect its function is particularly modern.

Chapter 4

FORM: FROM STATIC TO DYNAMIC

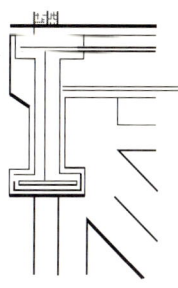

Great political revolutions have achieved the ascendancy of democracy. Technical development has expanded the nature of the knowable. The secularization of culture has transformed the subject matter of art into that which is individual and self-conscious. Yet, classically styled, if not classical, buildings are still being commissioned, designed, and constructed in all modes of architecture: residential, public, and commercial. What this implies is significant for the understanding of modernism.

Classicism as Image

An important part of what distinguished the ancient Greeks from other civilizations was their projection of human characteristics as their image of divine beings. Their art depicted the gods as looking like humans, living much like humans—albeit eternally—and relating with each other like humans. This personalization of the spiritual element in human thought is a defining characteristic of classical architecture.

For the gods lived in houses that were seen to be idealized versions of Greek wooden domestic architecture. Temples were constructed of marble, considered an eternal material but sculpted to represent the elements and joints of the wooden architecture upon which the stone temples were based. The temple form in classical architecture emphasizes important places such as churches, palaces, and government buildings.

The idealized house of the god is found, of course, in other cultures, including those of the Chinese and Mexican peoples. Ironically, it would seem, the degree to which the Greeks stretched this analogy throughout their culture is what generated Western humanism, the study of humankind living in the material world. Not the least aspect of democracy as it was practiced by the Greeks was the accessibility of these gods to each citizen. The personalization of religion disrupted the centralized power structure more typical of developing civilizations. It led to ideas of morality and behavior that were separate from religious belief and, especially, from political power.

The close depiction of the natural world and interest in the ordinary and everyday are what distinguish the Greek

Figure 67. Church of S. Giorgio Maggiore, Venice. Andrea Palladio, 1565.

culture, leading to humanism and democracy, the twin foundations of Western civilization. The controversy surrounding the depiction of naturalistic human figures in religious art arose from these trends, which are yet quite foreign and even offensive to many of the Islamic and Judaic sects. In view of the general secularization of culture in Western societies in the twentieth century, the concern of established religions is understandable.

Their admiration of Greek art and Greek political principles did not prevent the Romans from applying them in reestablishing a hegemony of power derived from a divine Emperor. The development of the classical image, therefore, suited those who sought to centralize political power. In this form classicism was quite different from the humanist, democratic ideal. On the one hand is a closed tradition, looking backward in time to a Golden Age and seeking to justify political action by its standards. On the other hand is an open-ended investigation of human life, experienced immediately by the individual. It is this latter emphasis that would, through the nineteenth century, eventually develop into what we know today as modernism.

Classicism as Art

The forms of classical architecture are based on the articulation of structure according to a hierarchical system of functional areas. The shapes themselves are derived from Greek and Roman models and sized according to strict proportions determined by history and mathematical theory. During the Renaissance, classical forms became codified. Both Alberti in the fifteenth century and Palladio in the sixteenth achieved a relationship between the articulation of the exterior and interior of buildings, which reinforced the unity of the classical system and at the same time abstracted it. The development and formalization of architectural drafting during the seventeenth and eighteenth centuries enhanced this abstracted quality.

At the time of the archeological discoveries of the remains of ancient buildings in Greece and Italy, historical fact met abstract theory and a split occurred. The archeological strain reclaimed the ancient forms and codified them in a representational manner different from that of the Renaissance. Just as the ancient Romans had applied the images of Greek humanism to an imperial government, the Ecole des Beaux-Arts and other academies applied them to the grand projects of oligarchic and commercial interests.

The Renaissance ideal of coherently designed structure, however, continued as a thread in the various revivals of the nineteenth century. Technological change finally forced the appearance of a totally new form of architecture. The visual equivalent of this may be termed *disjuncture,* a conscious expression of the separation of equivalent systems. Each system itself may be a regularly coordinated hierarchy of components, but its expression as a system must be unique and uncompromised by the larger whole. The single most essential distinction, then, between the classical and the modern is that between *hierarchical* and *heterarchical* systems, the latter being identified through the disjuncture of components. Disjuncture may be expressed not only in the physical parts of the building structure but also in functional elements and in what may be called cultural elements: the iconographic contents of the building, historically determined and formally derived. It is the very nature of classicism to express hierarchy—of parts, spaces, and functions—as well as balance and exclusivity—what is important and what is not. Modernism, in its reaction to classicism at the deepest level, has come to represent heterarchy, the interaction of parts,

FORM: FROM STATIC TO DYNAMIC

140

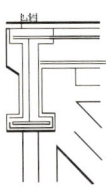

Figure 68. Palace of Fine Arts, San Francisco. Bernard Maybeck, 1915.

141

FORM:
FROM STATIC
TO
DYNAMIC

Figure 69. Casa del Girasole, Rome. Luigi Moretti, 1950.

spaces, and functions; dynamic imbalance; and the inclusion of all aspects of experience into the architectural continuum, whether they can be understood or not.

Disjuncture has been shown to be a key element in the work of Wright, Le Corbusier, and Alvar Aalto, but it is more than an invention of the great proto-modern designers. The notion of separated systems developed gradually in the vision of Western culture. It can be traced back as far as the Erechtheion in Periclean Athens, for that matter. But the importance of the disjunctured vision is in its role as a foundation for a new vision of art and culture. This gradually occurred throughout the nineteenth century and resulted in the profoundly new modern architecture of the twentieth.

It will be shown that disjuncture as a stylistic intention essentially denies the inevitably hierarchical organization of classical systems. Its appearance in modern and proto-modern works signals a rejection of the classical hegemony on the part of the designer. In consequence, disjuncture is a necessary and unique aspect of all modern styles, even a defining characteristic. This study establishes that modernism derives from a new view of order that is itself characterized by disjuncture. In the larger sense, it means a dynamic rather than a static order such as may be seen, for example, in the development of the two-party political system in the United States. The realization at the deepest level of our culture that this pattern of equivalent systems was in fact itself a comprehensive formal structure—rather than just a resistance to, or some transition between, classically based hierarchies—is the beginning of what must be called modernism. This is not to say that modern styles have nothing to do with classicism. Indeed, modernism appears as a denial of any ultimate hierarchy and thus includes some classical content, if only to refute it.

SPACE

When Michelangelo applied a giant order to the façade of the palaces on the Capitoline Hill in Rome in 1538, a major change in classical design occurred. For this action—not unique in Michelangelo's work—denied the Vitruvian system and detached the articulation of the building from the expression of structure. At the same time it increased the degree of hierarchy in the system by setting up a means for encompassing different levels of orders.

That this occurred in connection with the papal reconstruction of Rome is most significant, for it parallels the development of the new church of St. Peter's with its graded system of domes and vaults. The intention was to define the center of civilization at the residence of the Pope, in order to combat Protestant heresies and retain control of the church. Michelangelo's design for the central plaza of the Capitol with its antique statue of Marcus Aurelius was meant specifically to represent the continuity of Christian civilization through tradition.

During the eighteenth century, interest in the architecture of the Italian Renaissance succeeded the sensation of the rediscovery of antique architecture in Greece and Rome. Expeditions were arranged, measurements were taken, and a series of books, such as those by Paul Letarouilly in 1825, celebrated in a series of plates the great Renaissance palaces, churches, and plazas. These plates, like those of Stuart and Revett, were engraved and presented an abstract, technical depiction of the Renaissance monuments. The use of *poché* rendered an opposition of solid and void that was the basis for the classical sense of space.

In the modern era, the idea of disjunctured space—charged, dynamic, and positive—has developed as a more pertinent means of expressing the contemporary world. Modern

Figure 70. Richards Medical Laboratories, University of Pennsylvania. Louis Kahn, 1957–61.

143

FORM:
FROM STATIC
TO
DYNAMIC

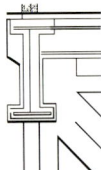

science has systematized such ideas as the magnetic lines of force around the earth, the existence and identification of gases in the atmosphere, the nature of light, and the mapping of the globe, all of which contribute to the denial of space as "nothingness." The classical notion of form as a solid in space, modeled by light and shadow, succumbs to a dualism of solid and void, both of which are energized and dynamic. Their interrelationship is not entirely definable in a modern space and must be represented by a collision or intersection of building elements shaped by forces defined through the design process. Modern space is thus expressed as disjunctured.

Space may act independently of form. An interior space may be laid out according to measurements that contradict those of the solid elements. In a building of classical style, such contradiction would be regularized, organized through articulation into a harmonious, cohesive composition. A modern space will define the collision as precisely as possible, without attempting to resolve it. The result in both cases is balance, but of a radically different nature.

When form responds to space, its classical relationship to space is destroyed and a new expression is created, problematic in perception. But part of the modern idea is that perception to some extent requires understanding in order to grasp the contemporary world. The lightness of modern construction, for example, expressed in cantilevered construction and the delicacy of glass curtain walls, allows space to define itself beyond its containing enclosure, independent of gravity.

Enclosure

Classical space is enclosed. Degrees of enclosure could be defined by the classical system. Colonnade, balustrade, arcade, loggia, and wall each specify a different degree of penetrability. The space is defined by the degree of penetrability of the wall. When Renaissance architects coordinated the interior and exterior articulation of systems, they codified this definition of space in a coherent way.

The modern idea of space is independent of enclosure. A ceiling plane, for example, can be delimited separately from the surrounding walls. In order to define a physical space, some concept of a virtual space must be generated by the imagination. This is then invoked by the lines and edges of surfaces, frequently layered in some manner established through the design process. The engagement of the imagination in this way produces the charged effect of modern space.

At the entrance to Louis Kahn's Richards Medical Laboratories, the strong diagonal axis overcomes the central axis formed naturally by the symmetrical building. Yet even this axis is denied by the impracticality of climbing a stair at the corner. One actually turns to the side and climbs orthogonally.

Some of this quality can be seen in an earlier, proto-modern entrance by another Philadelphia architect, Frank Furness. The entrance seems to be sliced right out of the block of the Thomas Hocklin House, which is then supported on comically trivial columns. An independent diagonal, this time vertical, is defined by the stair.

Importance of Screens

Part of the independence of space is the modern concept of screens. In classical architecture, screens were decorative elements, such as windows, used to fill enclosures but not a major determinant of the architectural effect. The modern view sees walls themselves as screening elements, independent of the support structure, that may define a space and also allow a space to penetrate them. The simultaneous occupation of material space by two opposing elements, one solid and one void, is what challenges and creates modern perception. Disjunctured space is the result.

Colin Rowe and Robert Slutzky, in their seminal essay

145

FORM:
FROM STATIC
TO
DYNAMIC

Figure 71. Entry, Richards Medical Laboratories, University of Pennsylvania. Louis Kahn, 1957–61.

146

Figure 72. Thomas Hocklin House, Philadelphia. Frank Furness, 1875.

147

FORM:
FROM STATIC
TO
DYNAMIC

Figure 73. Finlandia Hall, Helsinki. Alvar Aalto, 1971.

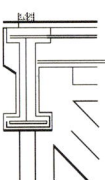

"Transparency, Literal and Phenomenal," correctly make a distinction between *literal* transparency—such as found in glass and perforated metal—and *phenomenal* transparency, which is an impression generated by spatial cues. The impression of phenomenal transparency is produced within the mind when it cannot resolve information it perceives in the material world.

Here we have reached the kernel of the great difference between modernism and classicism. A classical building is complete both materially and perceptually. Its evocative power comes from the identity between its presence and how it is perceived. The tectonic quality of fine classical work is generated by a perfect representation of material reality. One can sense the weight and substance without actually touching the surface, because the tectonic and visual perceptions are in perfect accord.

The modern work, on the other hand, is incomplete in its material self and requires the participation of the viewer to generate a perception. When a roof plane seems to hover independent of support, the mind in some way supplies a resolution in the form of some invisible but perceptible *force* that is the source of the dynamism of modern space. The degree to which this engagement is coherent with the nature of the work determines the quality of modern art.

Outside and Inside

The classical ideal of procession forms the basis for the ordering of degrees of enclosure. A formal sequence of gardens—*parterre, bosquet, selvatico*—bring one to the building, and then a series of scaled loggias and anterooms, depending on the grandeur of the structure, communicate the importance of the occasion and one's relative position in the scheme of things. Typically, the interior of a neoclassical room of the nineteenth century has little to do with the exterior. Contrary to Renaissance theory, classical architecture of the last two hundred years can be detailed and finished—even the shape of the openings—in a completely different manner inside than outside. The nature of classical space is in the clear differentiation between solid and void. The continuity of a structural system between inner and outer is not significant.

An entirely different conception is present in modern architecture. It is important that so many great modern works—those by Wright, Le Corbusier, Miës van der Rohe, Kahn, and Aalto—make a point of coordinating interior materials with the outer. This has been frequently seen as integrity of structure or honesty of materials in discussing modern design.

> The violations of truth, which dishonor poetry and painting, are thus for the most part confined to the treatment of their subjects. But in architecture another and a less subtle, more contemptible, violation of truth is possible; a direct falsity of assertion respecting the nature of material, or the quality of labor. And this is, in the full sense of the word, wrong; it has been a sign, wherever it has widely and with toleration existed, of a singular debasement of the arts; that it is not a sign worse than this, of a general want of severe probity, can be accounted for only by our knowledge of the strange separation which has for some centuries existed between the arts and all other subjects of human intellect, as matters of conscience. [1]

Heard throughout history, John Ruskin's argument for honesty in materials is one of the most common justifications of modernism. Henry-Russell Hitchcock titled his book on Frank Lloyd Wright *In the Nature of Materials*.

Furthermore, a sharpened attention to material reality signals a change in how matter is perceived. A wall is not just a surface but an *object in space*. A permanent continuity exists between inner and outer in the modern mind that is translated into a sense of material substance quite different from the classical solid-void opposition. Size and weight are no longer directly related, nor are solidity and opacity. The coherence of classical design is not possible for the disjunctured space of modernism.

Transparency

One of the elements of Japanese architecture that impressed the proto-modern architects was the sliding screens that made up the walls. Today, it requires concentration to realize how different this seemed to classically trained designers. The concept of a room was transformed into that of a *space*, a volume that was not permanent but changeable. The elements that could give definition to that volume—the columns, the screens, and the ceiling—were not necessarily coordinated at any given time. Thus, multiple impressions of what the space consisted of were perceivable simultaneously. This is not repose, but uncertainty.

The balance of modern architecture consists in the relative strength of opposing signals. One's perception should always be in a process of change. Buildings must be experienced in time. The material elements and one's idea about them are different things entirely, and both are necessary to modern art.

Typically, the surface of a classical wall is correctly rendered in three levels, corresponding to the base, shaft, and capital of the column. The structural system is further articulated by the texture of the masonry, the size and configuration of the stones, and the striking of the joints, if any. Piers and columns, half-round or full-round, can be developed from the wall or stand independently of it. This articulation is always clear and substantial, coordinated with the axis or centerline of the wall, inferred from its thickness. Openings in the wall reveal this thickness through the return of the material.

Sliding screens must, on the other hand, be offset to pass each other. They must also be offset from structural elements to slide past them as well. A series of layers is required which together make up the wall system. The abstraction of this idea from Japanese traditional architecture is its contribution to modern Western architecture. The layering of material as well as space is frequently reflected by detailing the return around an opening to reveal the thinness of the surface and the supporting structure beneath it.

GEOMETRY

The development of advanced techniques in geometry and mathematics did not lead to a modern architecture based on complex curves. Economic forces have dictated that the Cartesian solids would be as basic to modernism as they were to classicism. These are elements of the classical system incorporated into modern architecture. Late Baroque architecture did use ellipses and warped surfaces that were difficult to lay out and render, but the rendering of buildings remained two-dimensional based on plan, section, and elevation.

In the abstraction of modern form, shapes are independent of structure. This means that a circular opening in brick is not an arch. The upper half of the curve has no more significance than the lower half. The free-form cutouts of Le Corbusier's late architecture and circular and square openings in Louis Kahn's buildings dematerialize the wall, trivializing its structural role.

Cartesian Solids

The classical arrangement of the Cartesian solids is to align axes in a balanced symmetry. Modern design produces axes in conflict. The disparity between the perception of a building and its material presence is an active element in modern

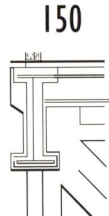

150

151

FORM:
FROM STATIC
TO
DYNAMIC

Figure 74. Entrance, Finlandia Hall, Helsinki. Alvar Aalto, 1971.

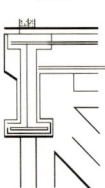

design. Gestalt psychology and other studies of perception have shown that Cartesian shapes generate their own presence. A portion of a circle implies the rest. In the mind, shapes can exist in the same place simultaneously. A modern space plays on this capacity to produce a dynamic effect by providing cues for coexisting Cartesian shapes.

Plasticity

The tectonic quality of classical architecture stems from its presentation of a visual image that is in conformance with the sense of touch and a kinesthetic sense of gravity or weight. The solid-void relationship is strict and clear. Surface effects such as roundness and depth of detail are revealed through shadows. The result is the coherent sensation of plasticity characteristic of classical architecture. It is rational because all of the senses are in agreement.

Modern architecture seeks a radically different experience. A modern building is in a certain sense an incomplete representation of its generating drawings, themselves an analysis of a mental state. Consider the composite, cubistic quality of Le Corbusier's houses or the linear lucidity of the space in a Wright house. The bronze mullions of the Seagram Building were rolled in a shape designed to give a sharp line, equivalent to the precision of the drawing of a technical pen. They are linear rather than tactile.

Substance and Lightness

Classical buildings are weighty. They gain their effect from shapes that are in accord with readily understandable structural principles. The buttresses of a dome, its associated pendentives, arches, and piers are clear about the transfer of load from the span to the earth.

Modern architecture is planar rather than plastic. It has an essential lightness that makes the bearing of weight a trivial matter. Its shapes are abstract and nonrepresentational. The famous Dom-Ino prototype for housing generated by Le Corbusier shows the essential modern space. It is defined by a ground plane and a roof plane. The supports are inconsequential, the minimum that is needed. The stair is an exposed construction and seems to be unsupported. The point is that it is in fact supported and a comprehensive perception of the space must include an element supplied by the imagination of the perceiver. The material by itself presents an incomplete picture.

Plane, Slab, and Surface

The techniques of construction of classical buildings were based on the cutting, carving, and placing of masonry. Thus, the drums of stone that are assembled to make a column are closely joined and detailed to diminish the actual joint. Rusticated masonry reveals the joint in a controlled way, usually by a smooth recessed reveal at the edges of the blocks. This produces a shadow that supports the expression of depth and weight in a way that a surface line cannot. Lines in classical architecture are expressed as the edges of a solid, as corners.

Modern architecture addresses the joining of construction elements in a completely different way. The line itself is paramount, and the way it is expressed as a construction element is part of the discourse of modern design. The interaction of geometry and construction elucidates the relationship between the mental and the material, the ideal and the real.

In the classical system, the surface is an indivisible part of the solid-void duality. Perception of the surface is tectonic as well as visual, and these are in accord. The modern system abstracts the plane, representing it in slabs of certain material thickness. The slab derives from the plane, where the classical surface derives from its solid.

153

FORM:
FROM STATIC
TO
DYNAMIC

Figure 75. School of Architecture, Rice University. James Stirling, 1984.

Coordination of Systems

The classical expression of harmony stems from geometric integration and a hierarchy of measurement and dimension, according to a clear system of proportion. A hierarchy of importance is established, defined by symmetry, axiality, and scale. Large, important shapes are placed in the center, and smaller, subordinate elements at the sides.

The modern expression is dynamic. It expresses a series of systems established in a sequence that starts with the initial ideas about the building, follow through the designing and detailing, and is complete only with the elements of construction. The abstraction of the system of measurement may be expressed as an independent element that collides unpredictably with structural and material systems in the building. For example, the joints in the sidewalks at Florida Southern College by Wright are not necessarily related to the direction of the sidewalk. Part of the detailing procedure for Wright's Usonian houses was to pick up construction joints from a grid impressed in the concrete floor slab. Lines can be seen to pass from material to material independent of the actual joints between the systems.

ORGANIZATION

Although based on Cartesian sources, the typical plan of a classical building does not generally follow a perfect grid. The equal spacing of columns and arches does tend to call for regularity in the plan, but adjustments are almost always made to allow for different room sizes and shapes or to enable a more complete plastic expression of classical shapes. The corner where two arcades are joined is a famous example of the latter. The plasticity of the classical system is foremost, and the underlying grid is adjusted as necessary.

Modern buildings are typically determined strictly according to multiple grids that express forces from the design process that have shaped the building. The interaction of structural frame and curtain wall is an example. The greater the independence of the grids, the better is the expression of disjunctured space. Alvar Aalto's work displays freely formed shapes determined by circulation, daylighting, building services and structure, each of which is laid out according to an independent grid: rectangular, radial, or otherwise.

Streets and Site Planning

Façades of classical buildings feature masonry walls with grilled openings at street level, or even colonnades or arcades as on the Rue de Rivoli in Paris. When united behind a coherent façade, as at the Crescent at Bath, the buildings are subservient to the expression of civic harmony. But more typically, different classically styled fronts abut each other without mutual response. The details of classical buildings are repeated in the coordinated benches, lampposts, paving, and other elements of the streetscape. The look of the street can be kept in scale with the adjoining buildings.

Modern buildings tend to connect or unite with the street at pedestrian level through transparent lobbies. The International Style tower on a plaza is the archetype for modern planning. Le Corbusier's famous city plans added a dynamic vertical element to what had been two-dimensional and ground-based.

MODULE

Regularization of the bay is natural for an architecture of round arches. The similarity in height determines a similarity in length and width. Classical architecture is structurally modular in this sense. Brunelleschi in fourteenth century Florence appeared to be interested in modular architecture in

155

FORM:
FROM STATIC
— TO —
DYNAMIC

Figure 76. Technical University, Otaniemi, Finland. Alvar Aalto, 1964.

a way that seems almost modern. The effect of repeated identical bays is very strong in his churches, San Lorenzo and Santo Spirito.

This sense of what modern architects would call the module was passed from Gothic styles, which incorporated repeated structural bays in a consciously spatial way. The ambulatories of large churches presented a series of chapels, frequently organized in procession. Multiples were an important part of Gothic architecture: the twelve apostles and the stations of the cross are just two examples of the many variations on multiples found in the Bible. The structural flexibility of the Gothic system of vaulting naturally supported this iconography.

After Brunelleschi, however, classical styles developed in a hierarchical rather than multiple format. The centrality of the dome tended to suppress the repeating quality of Gothic design that would be termed modular today. Michelangelo's giant order, mentioned earlier, provides the definitive classical organization: greater to lesser. The looseness and adaptability of Gothic architecture was scorned as barbaric by classical writers.

The fitness of Gothic styles for modern techniques of framing and support was one of the main reasons for the Gothic Revival of the nineteenth century. Viollet-le-Duc and John Ruskin were only two of many influential proponents of the combination. The resurgence of modularity can be seen as early as the Crystal Palace of 1851.

Modern construction is precisely calculated for load-bearing capacity, and the economy of prefabrication and standardized shapes increases the modularity of contemporary design. However, the concept of modularity—an indeterminate whole generated by adding identical modules—is modern. The abstract quality of contemporary buildings is quite different from the symbolism incorporated in Gothic churches.

The Building Unit

Modularity in modern structures can be achieved by repeating identical bays, which is usually the most economic means of construction. The exterior wall and its openings and interior finishes are usually related to the bay in a subordinate manner that is classical, although the interaction of different modules imposed upon each other is a more consciously modern way of detailing. The work of Aalto has already been mentioned as a supreme example of this, but Wright and Le Corbusier have also based their architecture on this idea.

Another way of expressing a structural module is through prefabricated units, such as Moshe Safdie's Habitat in Montreal or some of Paul Rudolph's projects. The sense of indeterminate growth is very strong in work such as this. Le Corbusier's *Unité d'habitation* prototype combined independent modules with a containing support frame. The Lloyds of London headquarters by Richard Rodgers is another example.

The Functional Unit

There are many examples of repeated rows of attached houses with classical detailing, but it would be stretching to call this typical of the classical style. It is probably more accurate to say that modern architecture developed in part to express this aspect of classical residences. Middle-class and working-class housing only rarely managed to attract the attention of important classical architects. There is a strangely combined Utopian/Empire style found in some works of Ledoux that for some reason inspired certain architects in recent years, but one would be hard-pressed to detect any element of humanism in it.

Modern architecture addresses the functional unit from a scientific point of view, using the minimum sizes, clearances, and measurements established by various regulations and standards. In office buildings, workstations are standardized according to rank and when they are coordinated with the

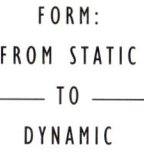

FORM:
FROM STATIC
TO
DYNAMIC

Figure 77. Lever House, Manhattan. Skidmore, Owings and Merrill, 1952. Still a classic of modern design, its clarity is emphasized by its grotesque new neighbor.

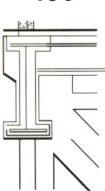

structural grid, achieve the controlled order of classical design. Hierarchically controlled corporations look favorably on such design. But the open workstation derives from the *Burolandschaft* movement of the 1960s in Germany, which sought to liberate the modern workplace from bureaucracy. The original designs were freely configured from standardized parts, and readily changeable to suit the needs of the individual worker.

There will always be those for whom the classical style provides a comfort, a predictability, and a tactility that is difficult to find in modernism. Anyone who believes that some people are better than others will find confirmation in classical design. Anyone who seeks to control opinion or impose authority upon others will find classicism useful.

Yet the birth of democracy is associated with the classical age of Greece, and the development of humanism included the revival of classical styles in the Renaissance. The beauty, simplicity, and order of classical buildings is a magnificent human achievement, the finest coordinated architecture that has ever been produced. Its power of inspiration resonates in the memory of Western civilization.

The issue for contemporary architects is whether the elements of classicism that are still relevant in the late twentieth century can best be expressed in a reference to classical forms or in the modernism that developed from them. Louis Sullivan's best work includes magnificent examples of a clear vision of the classical ideal and how it can address the modern world.

Figure 78. Condict Building, Manhattan. Louis Sullivan, 1898.

NOTES

Introduction

1. John Summerson, "The Mischievous Analogy" (1947, reprint in *Heavenly Mansions and Other Essays on Architecture* [New York: W. W. Norton, 1963]), p. 196.
2. Ada Louise Huxtable, "Inventing American Reality," *New York Review of Books* 39, no. 20 (December 1992): 24.
3. Thomas Jefferson, "Letter to Major Pierre Charles L'Enfant," April 10, 1791, in *The Portable Thomas Jefferson*, ed. Merrill D. Peterson (New York: Viking Penguin, 1975).
4. James S. Ackerman, *The Architecture of Michelangelo*, 2nd ed. (Chicago: University of Chicago Press, 1986), p. 138.

Chapter 1

1. John Ruskin, *The Seven Lamps of Architecture* (1849; reprint, New York: Farrar, Straus and Giroux, 1981), pp. 119–20. [8th printing]
2. Edith Wharton and Ogden Codman, Jr., *The Decoration of Houses* (New York: W. W. Norton, 1978), p. 23.
3. Aldo Rossi, *The Architecture of the City* (Cambridge, Mass.: Institute for Urban Studies and Architecture and the MIT Press, 1984), p. 21.
4. Sigfried Giedion, *Space, Time and Architecture: The Growth of a New Tradition* (1941; reprint, Cambridge, Mass.: Harvard University Press, 1978), p. lvi.
5. Wharton and Codman, *Decoration of Houses*, p. 189.
6. Ralph Waldo Emerson, "The American Scholar: An Oration Delivered Before the Phi Beta Kappa Society, at Cambridge, August 31, 1837," in *The American Tradition in Literature*, vol. 1, ed. Sculley Bradley, Richmond Croom Beatty, E. Hudson Long, and George Perkins (New York: Grosset and Dunlap, 1974), pp. 1089–90.
7. John Loring, design director of Tiffany & Company, quoted in "Profiles: Giving Good Value" by Holly Brubach, *The New Yorker*, August 10, 1992, pp. 56–57.
8. Wharton and Codman, *Decoration of Houses*, p. 31.
9. Wharton and Codman, *Decoration of Houses*, p. 34.
10. Colin Rowe and Robert Slutzky, "Transparency: Literal and Phenomenal," in *The Mathematics of the Ideal Villa and Other Essays*, Colin Rowe, ed. (Cambridge, Mass.: MIT Press, 1976), p. 175.
11. Ralph Waldo Emerson, "Nature," in *The American Tradition in Literature*, vol. 1, ed. Sculley Bradley, Richard Croom Beatty, E. Hudson Long, and George Perkins (New York: Grosset and Dunlap, 1974), pp. 1069–70.
12. John Ruskin, *Seven Lamps of Architecture*, pp. 37–38.

Chapter 2

1. D'Arcy Wentworth Thompson, *On Growth and Form* (1917; abridged edition, ed. John Tyler Bonner [New York: Cambridge University Press, 1961]), p. 5.
2. John Ruskin, *The Seven Lamps of Architecture* (New York: Farrar, Straus and Giroux, 1981), p. 39. [8th printing]
3. Robert Venturi; Denise Scott-Brown; and Steven Izenour, *Learning From Las Vegas: The Forgotten Symbolism of Architectural Form* (Cambridge, Mass.: MIT Press, 1977), p. 87.
4. Thompson, *On Growth and Form*, p. 11.
5. Sigfried Giedion, *Space, Time and Architecture: the Growth of a New Tradition* (1941; reprint, Cambridge, Mass.: Harvard University Press, 1978), p. 31.
6. John Summerson, "The Mischievous Analogy" (1947; reprint in *Heavenly Mansions and other Essays on Architecture* [New York: W. W. Norton, 1963]), p. 213.

Chapter 3

1. Edith Wharton and Ogden Codman, Jr., *The Decoration of Houses* (New York: W. W. Norton, 1978), p. 92.
2. Wharton and Cogman, *Decoration of Houses*, p. 189.
3. Frank Lloyd Wright, "In the Cause of Architecture," *The Architectural Record*, 23, no. 3 (1908; reprinted in *In the Cause of Architecture*, ed. Frederick Gutheim [New York: The Architectural Record]), p. 53.
4. D'Arcy Thompson, *On Growth and Form* (1917; abridged edition, ed. John Tyler Bonner [New York: Cambridge University Press, 1961], pp. 10–11.
5. Wharton and Codman, *Decoration of Houses*, p. 24.
6. D'Arcy Thompson, *On Growth and Form*, p. 3.
7. John Summerson, "The Mischievous Analogy" (1947, reprint in *Heavenly Mansions and Other Essays on Architecture* [New York: W. W. Norton, 1963]), pp. 205–206.
8. Christian Norberg-Shulz, *Late Baroque and Rococo Architecture* (New York: Abrams, 1974).
9. Henry-Russell Hitchcock and Philip Johnson, *The International Style* (1932; reprint, New York: W. W. Norton, 1966), p. 13.
10. Wharton and Codman, *Decoration of Houses*, p. 13.
11. Wharton and Codman, *Decoration of Houses*, p. 19.
12. Wharton and Codman, *Decoration of Houses*, p. 59.

Chapter 4

1. John Ruskin, *The Seven Lamps of Architecture* (New York: Farrar, Straus and Giroux, 1981), p. 38. [8th printing]

INDEX

Page numbers in italics indicate figures.

Aalto, Alvar
  Baker House by, *75*, 77
  disjuncture and, 142
  Finlandia Hall by, *147, 150–151*
  Technical University by, 154, *155*
  University Library by, *99*
abstraction
  of building materials, 88
  Cartesian solids and, 121
  design and, 21–22
  ornamentation vs., 88
  tempered interiors and, 78
Ackerman, James S., 7
airships
  weight concept and, 69, *72*
Alberti, Leon Battista
  exterior-interior articulation by, 139
American Revolution, 19, 31
American Telephone & Telegraph Building, New York, 107, *109*
Ames Library, North Easton, Mass., *90, 91*, 92
approach
  in classical architecture, 53–54
  control of, 47, 53
Arc de Triomphe, Paris, 34
arch
  intellectualization of, 88–92
  in Mayan civilization, 88
  structural vs. symbolic, 86, 92
archaeological discovery
  classical codification through, 31, 34, 139
  neoclassicism and, 102
architect
  building craft and, 29

  in building process, 30
  intention of, 16, 18
architectural drawings
  building construction and, 46–47, 67
  classical design and, 22
  collections of, 88
  design abstraction and, 21–22
  façade rendering in, 46–47
  reproduction of, 88
  technological advances in, 88
architectural elements
  classical incorporation of, 6
  coordination of systems in, 31–32
  equivalent systems in, 6
Architectural Record, 22
architecture. *See also* classical architecture; modern architecture
  general vs. specialized knowledge and, 19
  history and, 19–64
Architecture of the City, The, 23, 66
arcuated architecture, 77
art
  classicism and, 107
  subject matter of, 120
art history
  evolution of styles in, 125
Attia, Eli
  Hotel Macklowe by, *110*
auditorium, 58
  church as, 60
autocracy
  classicism and, 64, 102, 139
avant-garde, 2
axiality
  in campus planning, 129–134

  classical vs. modern, 46, 47, 53–54
    procession vs. circulation and, 128–129
  symmetry and, 46

Baker House, Massachusetts Institute of Technology, *75*, 77
Bank of England
  Hellenic Doric order of, 104
Baroque
  giant order in, 7, 12
basilica
  Roman, 37
Beaux-Arts Paris Opera, 12
Beth Sholom Synagogue, Philadelphia, 117
Borromini, Francesco, 120
  Oratorio of S. Filippo Neri by, 102, *106*
Brasilia, Brazil, 23
bronze
  in Seagram Building, 58
Brunelleschi, Filippo
  modular architecture and, 154, 156
brutalist style, 30
building codes, 31
building forms
  solid, 20
building materials
  evolution of, 25
  industrialization of, 88
  interior-exterior coordination of, 148–149
  plasticity of, 29–30
building systems. *See also* coordination of systems

  classical hierarchy in, 34–35
  coordination of, 31–37, 65
  equivalence in, 34–35
  independent, 65
building unit
  industrialized construction and, 57
  modularity in, 156
  steel/reinforced concrete and, 100
Bulfinch, Charles
  Massachusetts State House by, *63*, 64
  Old Meeting House by, 60, *61*, 62
Burnham, Daniel
  City Beautiful movement and, 20–21, 107
  Columbian Exhibition of 1893 and, 105
  railroad station plans by, 128
Burolandschaft movement, 158

Calder, Andrew, 124
Cambridge University, England
  tutorial system of, 134
Campidoglio, Rome
  Lincoln Center and, 7–16
  Palazzo dei Senatori of, *10*
  Palazzo Nuovo of, *8, 14*
campus planning, 129–134
Capital
  at Rome, 12, 64
  at Washington, D. C., 5, 54
Capitoline Hill, Rome
  giant order and, 142
Carson Pirie Scott department store, 57
Cartesian grid, 43, 94

Cartesian solids
  abstraction of, 88, 121
  classical vs. modern usage of, 28–29, 86
  cultural influences on, 121–122
  evolution of arch and, 88, 92
  industrialization and, 86, 88
  perception and, 149, 152
  technical drawing and, 88
  two-dimensional expression of, 86
Casa del Fascio, Como, 46
Casa del Girasole, Rome, *141*
catenary curve, 28
cathedrals
  High Gothic, 20
cave
  arcuated architecture and, 77
CBS Building, New York, 27, *28*, 122
Central Park, New York, 42
Chandigarh, India, 23
Chicago, Ill.
  modern architecture development and, 20
Church of S. Giorgio Magiore, Venice, *138*
churches
  as auditorium, 60
  equivalence vs. hierarchy in, 60–64
  outside-inside distinction in, 117, 120
  sacredness of
    classical vs. modern expression of, 117, 120
  structural interplay in, 60–64
circulation
  Beaux Arts planning of, 54
  concept of space and, 83
  modern planning for, 54, 128–129
  against symmetrical axes, 124
Citicorp Center, New York, *127*
cities
  classical
    zoning and, 128
  large-scale development and, 21
  modern architecture development and, 20–21
  orientation of, 98
City Beautiful movement
  on Broadway, Manhattan, 107, *108*
  function and, 104
  James J. Farley Post Office and, 35
  as utopian ideal, 20

city planning, 42–43, 46. *See also* site planning; street planning
  classical orders in, 43
  grids for, 43, 94
Civil War, 19–20
Classic Revival
  Columbian Exposition of 1893 and, 105, 107
  Lincoln Center and, 12
  University of Virginia plan and, 129
classical
  definition of, 2
  modern vs., 2–3
classical architecture. *See also* classicism
  architectural drawing and, 22
  axiality of, 46, 47, 53–54
  building technology in, 12, 152
  Cartesian solids in, 28–29, 86
  circulation in, 54
  climate influence on, 25
  coordination of, 53–54
  coordination of systems in, 31–32, 65
  detailing of, 27, *36*, 37, *38*, *39*, 57
  enclosure in, 22–23, 67, 144
  forms of, 139
  frontality of, 46, 98
  grid in, 154
  hierarchy of systems in, 34–35, 57, 60, 64, 104–105, 139, 142
  integration in, 7
  Lincoln Center as, 12, 14
  material-perceptual completeness of, 53, 148
  model adaptation in, 31
  modularity in, 98, 154, 156
  movement through, 54
  nature and, 24
  organization of, 34
  parts vs. whole in, 28–29
  perception and, 53
  perception of nature and, 47
  permanence of, 122
  plan of, 154
  plasticity of, 152
  primary vs. subsidiary spaces in, 22
  proportion in, 43, 46, 102–103
  social hierarchy in, 25–26
  solid and void in, 21, 83, 122, 148

spatial organization in, 26–27, 37, 42, 66, 144
  square in, 43, 46
  structural interplay in, 60, 64
  structural standards of, 77–78
  structural system of, 27, 57, 60, 64
  tactility of, 35, 121
  tectonics of, 92, 148, 152
  walls in, 27, 30, 149
  weight of, 67, 69, 83, 121, 152
  workplace and, 24
classical bay, 125
classical elements
  modern incorporation of, 2, 3, 6
classical ideal
  modernism and, 4
  procession in, 148
  of space, 21
classicism. *See also* classical architecture
  as art, 139–142
  autocracy and, 102
  as closed tradition, 139
  contemporary, 114
    intellectualization of culture and, 3
  democracy and, 5–6, 102
  denial of, 6, 60, 65, 142
  development of, 18, 20
  exclusiveness of, 6, 22–23
  function of, 3–4
  harmony in, 104
  hierarchy of, 34–35, 57, 60, 64, 104–105, 117
    vs. heterarchy, 139, 142
  as humanist democratic ideal, 137, 139
  as image, 137, *138*, 139
  modernism vs., 5, 6
  parts and orders in, 31
  reference to past in, 35, *36*, 37
  spiritual personification in, 137
  tenets of, 20
climate
  Western architecture and, 25
Codman, Ogden, Jr., 22, 30, 43, 46, 101, 102, 104, 117, 121, 124
Colonial Williamsburg, Va.
  themed artifact and, 4
Colonnade Row, New York, 43, *44–45*
Columbian Exposition of 1893, Chicago
  cultural change and, 105

landscape gardening of, 42
  neoclassicism and, 5, 20
  street planning and, 128
Condict Building, New York, *158*
Congrès Internationaux d'architecture moderne (CIAM), 20
conic sections, 28
construction
  abstraction of, 30
  craft vs., 30, 57
  enclosure and, 67
  layered technique of, 66
  lightness of, 83
  modularity in, 156
  weight and, 67, 69
coordination
  classical vs. modern, 53–54
coordination of systems
  in classical vs. modern architecture, 31–37, 65
  cultural effects on, 124–125
  dynamic balance in, 124
  form and, 154
  harmony in, 124–125, 154
  in James J. Farley Post Office, 32–33, 35, 37
  in Main Post Office, Chicago, 35, *36*, 37, *38*
  modern expression of, 154
  symmetry in, 124
  technologic advances and, 92, 94
  in U. S. Office, Philadelphia, 37, *39*
Corbusier Revival
  Lincoln Center and, 7
craft
  of building, 30, 57
Crane Memorial Library, Quincy, Mass., 92, *93*
Crystal Palace
  accessibility to, 25
  independent space and, 26
  modularity and, 156
  railroad stations based on, 128
cubism
  classicism and, 115
  modern architecture and, 22
culture, 102–136
  axiality and, 128–134
  Cartesian solids and, 121–122
  change of scale and, 101–136
  circulation of ideas and, 101
  coordination of systems and, 124–125

development of architectural
     representation in, 105–114
  dynamic form and, 122
  enclosure and, 115–117
  exclusion/inclusion and, 120
  geometry and, 120–125
  intellectualization of, 3, 20
  modernism definition and, 102–114
  modularity and, 134–136
  organizational influences of,
     125–134
  outside-inside distinction and,
     117–120
  ownership and, 120
  plasticity and, 122–124
  privacy and, 115–117
  shelter and, 117
  space and, 114–120
  street/site planning and, 125–128
  tectonics and, 121–122
  virtual space and, 124

Darwin, Charles, 66, 125
Darwin Martin House, Buffalo, 46
Davenport College, Yale University,
     78, *80–81*
decoration
  carving vs. reproduction of, 122
Decoration of Houses, The, 22, 30, 43,
     46, 101, 102, 104, 117, 121, 124
democracy
  classicism and, 102
  enclosure and, 115
  individual vs. whole in, 29
  modernism and, 5–6, 19, 64
  public building design and, 5
Descartes, René, 86
design
  abstraction and, 21–22
  independence of building systems
     in, 65
  intellectualization in, 47
  intuition vs. intellect in, 66
  scientific application of
     ancient models and, 19
  technological advances and, 94
  two-dimensional, 67
  unpredictability in, 28
detailing
  classical vs. modern, 34, *36*, 37, *38,
     39*, 57
  mechanization effect on, 35

disjuncture, 6, 53
  conservative classicism and, 111
  definition of, 139
  expression of, 139, 142
  independence of grids and, 154
  independent building systems and,
     65
  multiculturalism and, 114
  screens in, 144
Disney Enterprises, 4
dissociation
  building-axis, 53
  size-support, 121–122
Dulles Airport, Chantilly, Va., 77, *79*
dynamic balance, 53, 83, 104, 122, 124

Ecole des Beaux-Arts
  architectural drawings and, 88
  circulation and, 54
  City Beautiful movement and, 107
  city plans of, 43
  classical forms and, 139
  enclosure and, 22
  James J. Farley Post Office and, 35
  modernism and, 20
  planning grid of, 94
  separation of function and, 22
  solid-void quality and, 122
  two-dimensional planning in, 67
economics
  orientation and, 98
  site planning and, 94, *95–97*, 98
Eiffel Tower, Paris, 35
Einstein, Albert, 107
Embarcadero, San Francisco, *95*
Emerson, Ralph Waldo, 31, 47
enclosure
  classical, 22–23, 67, 144
  climatic effects on, 25
  cultural effects on, 115–117
  dynamism of, 67
  exclusivity vs. inclusivity in, 22–23
  form and, 144–148
  frames and, 69–77
  functionality of, 67
  membranes and, 77
  modern, 23–25, 67–77, 144
  nature and, 23–24
  outside-inside distinction in, 25–26
  privacy and, 115, 117
  in private/public places, 24–25
  screens and, 144–148

shelter and, 117
  social interaction and, 25–26
  transparency and, 149
  walls and, 67–69, 115, *116*
engineer
  building craft and, 29
Enlightenment period
  geometry and, 27
environment
  in modern architecture, 23
  orientation and, 98
equivalency, 34–35, 124
  of building elements, 6
  in churches, 60–64
  disjuncture in, 139
European culture
  modern architecture development
     and, 20
  traditional culture and, 6
expressionism, 78

façade
  classical vs. modern articulation of,
     55, 56, 57, 122
  unfinished vs. formal, 46–47
factory
  as functional unit, 57
Farnese Palace, Rome, 92
fasteners, 92
Federal Reserve Bank, New York, 104
Finlandia Hall, Helsinki, *147, 150–151*
Florida Southern College, 129, 134,
     154
force
  modern architecture and, 83, *84, 85,*
     86, 103–104, 148
form, 137–158
  building unit and, 156
  of Cartesian solids, 149–152
  of classicism, 137–142
  coordination of systems and, 154
  enclosure and, 144–148
  force and
     in modernism definition, 103–104
  functional unit and, 156–158
  geometry and, 149–154
  modularity and, 154–158
  organization and, 154, *155*
  outside-inside distinction and,
     148–149
  planar, 152
  plasticity and, 152–153

as solid and void, 144
  space and, 142–149
  street-site planning and, 154
  transparency and, 149
framed architecture, 77
frames
  classical, 69, *75*
  modern, 69, *75*, 77
  structural expression and, 78
French Revolution, 19, 31
Freud, Sigmund, 107
frontality, 46, 98
function
  compartmentalization of, 22
functional unit
  historical change in, 57–58
  modern expression of, 156, 158
functionalism, 30–31
Furness, Frank
  Library, University of Pennsylvania
     by, *123*, 124
  Thomas Hocklin House by, 144, *146*

Geer, Seth
  Colonade Row, Manhattan by, 43,
     44–45
*Genius Loci: Towards a Phenomenology
  of Architecture*, 66
geometry. *See also* coordination of
     systems
  architectural applications of, 86
  architectural drawings and, 88
  Cartesian. *See* Cartesian grid;
     Cartesian solids
  classical, 86, 120
  cultural effects on, 120–125
  form and, 149–154
  functionalism and, 30–31
  logic and, 27
  in mathematical analysis, 86
  in modern architecture
     development, 27–37
  in modern forms, 149
  in modular building, 86, *87*
  plasticity and, 29–30, 92, 122, 124,
     152
  prefabrication and, 86
  proportion and, 120–121
  size and scale in, 29
  systems of measurement in, 27–28
  technologic advances and, 86–94
giant order, 7, 12, 34

INDEX

Giedion, Sigfried, 26–27, 88
Giurgola, Romaldo
    Penn Mutual Life Building by, 125, *126*
glass
    dynamic quality of, 27
    modern style and, 7, 12
    outside-inside distinction and, 78
    walls of, 77
Gmelin & Walker
    Irving Trust Company by, *113*
Golden Mean, 46, 86, 121
Goodyear Blimp, 69, 72
Gothic architecture
    climate influence on, 25
    modularity in, 156
    space and, 20
Gothic Revival, 5, 21, 77–78
    codification of, 34
    modularity in, 156
    at Yale University, 78, *80–81*
Government Services Center, Boston, 69, *73*
Grad Partnership
    Richard Hughes Justice Complex by, 69, *74*
Grand Central Station, New York, 128
Greek civilization
    divine personification in, 137
    human naturalistic depiction in, 139
    understanding vs. experiencing of, 3
Greek Revival, 34
greenbelt, 98
grid
    multiple, 154, *155*

Hallidie Building, San Francisco, *76*
Hardy House, Racine, Wis., 46
harmony
    classical, 124–125, 154
    Darwin and, 125
    dynamic expression of, 154
Harrison & Abramovitz
    Philharmonic Hall, Lincoln Center by, *11, 14*
Harvard University, Cambridge, Mass.
    Sever Hall at, 105
Hatch Act (1887)
    campus planning and, 129
Haussmann plan, Paris, 57
    City Beautiful movement and, 107
    processional quality of, 128

Heavenly Mansions and other Essays on Architecture, 92, 94, 105
heterarchy, 139, 142
hierarchy
    in churches, 60–64
    classical, 34–35, 57, 60, 64, 104–105, 139, 142
    denial of, 6, 60, 65, 142
    polyarchy vs., 124
    scale and, 64
    of workstation, 156, 158
High Gothic cathedrals, 20
High Renaissance
    giant order in, 7, 12
highways
    expression of motion and, 83, *84*
history
    modernist architecture and, 19–64
Hitchcock, Henry-Russell, 7, 114, 148
Hobson, Henry, 67, *68*, 70
Hotel Macklowe, New York, *110*
house
    family structure and, 115, 117
    as functional unit, 57–58
    mechanistic view of, 66
    monument vs.
        growth of democracy and, 29
    planning unit for, *132–133*, 134, 136
Houses of Parliament, London, 54
humanism
    Renaissance art and, 114
Huxtable, Ada Louise, 4

I Quattro Libri, 120
iconoclasm, 4
Il Redentore, Venice, 69, *75*
Illinois Institute of Technology, Chicago
    Chemistry Building at, *131*, 134
    Crown Hall at, *130*, 134
impressionism
    classicism and, 115
In the Nature of Materials, 148
independent space, 20
individual
    within society, 19, 31
industrialization
    modernist architecture and, 19–20
    relation to nature in, 24
    work transformation and, 24
Inland Steel Building, Chicago, *135*, 136

interiors
    tempering of, 78
International Style, 3, 20
    1930 Museum of Modern Art show on, 111
    Brasilia and, 23
    City Beautiful movement and, 107
    façade articulation in, 57
    Frank Lloyd Wright and, 107
    large-scale development and, 21
    Lincoln Center and, 7, 12
    Main Post Office, Chicago and, 35
    Penn Station and, 23
    Rockefeller Center and, 60
    Seagram Building and, 58
    space perception in, 27
    streetscape in, 154
    structure and, 78
International Style, The, 7, 114
Irving Trust Company, New York, *113*
Italian Renaissance
    architecture of, 142
Izenour, Steven, 78

James J. Farley Post Office, New York, *32–33*, 35, 37, 69, 111
    structure of, 122
Japanese architecture
    influence on Frank Lloyd Wright by, 107, 111, 117
    modular design in, 42
    sliding screens in, 149
jazz
    classicism and, 107
Jefferson, Thomas, 5, 18, 29, 105
    University of Virginia plan by, 129
Johnson, Philip, 7, 114
    New York State Theater, Lincoln Center by, *9*
joints
    in modern vs. classical architecture, 152, 154
Judge Building, New York, 67, *71*

Kahn, Louis
    Richards Medical Laboratories by, *143*, 144
    wall openings of, 149
Kresge Auditorium
    at Massachusetts Institute of Technology, 16

landmarks preservation movement, 2
landscape
    zoning and, 128
landscape gardening, 42
Late Baroque
    space and, 20
Late Baroque and Rococo Architecture, 114
Late Baroque Revival
    University of Virginia plan and, 129
Le Corbusier, Charles-Edouard Jeanneret, 23
    churches of, 117
    conception of house by, 66
    disjuncture in, 142
    dissociation and, 53
    Dom-Ino prototype of, 152
    economy of designs and, 111
    free-form cutouts of, 149
    International Style and, 111
    modern dwellings and, 24
    Modulor system of measurement and proportion of, 27, 46, 121
    phenomenal transparency and, 47
    plasticity and, 152
    two-dimensional planning and, 67
    Unité d'Habitation of, 98, 100, 125, 156
Learning from Las Vegas, 78
Letarouilly, Paul, 142
Lever House, New York, *157*
Library, University of Pennsylvania, *123*, 124
Lincoln Center, New York
    Campidoglio and, 7–16
    classical content of, 12, 14
    detailing of, 35
    empire-building aspects of, 14
    Metropolitan Opera House of, *11*, 30
    modern style of, 7, 12
    New York State Theater of, *9, 13*
    Philharmonic Hall of, 12, 14, *14*
    Sydney Opera House and, 16
    as urban renewal, 14
    Vivian Beaumont Repertory Theater of, *15*
literature
    classicism and, 107
Loos, Adolf, 88
Loring, John, 34
Louvre, Paris, 53

INDEX

machine age, 30
Main Post Office, Chicago, 35, *36*, 37, *38*, 65, 111
Manhattan, New York
    commercial block in, *49*
    loft building in, *50–52*
masonry
    framing of, 69, 77, 78
    solid and void and, 83
Massachusetts Institute of Technology, Cambridge
    Baker House at, *75*, 77
    Kresge Auditorium at, 16
Massachusetts State House, Boston, *63*, 64
mathematics
    modernization of, 120–121
Mayan civilization
    arch in, 88
Maybeck, Bernard
    Palace of Fine Arts by, *140*
McKim, Mead & White, 21
    City Beautiful movement and, 107
    James J. Farley Post Office by, *32–33*, 35, 37, 111
    Judge Building by, 67, *71*
    Municipal Building by, 92
    street planning and, 128
    U.S. Capitol and, 5
measurement. *See also* Cartesian solids; coordination of systems; geometry
    abstraction of, 154
mechanization, 30
    effect on detailing of, 35
membrane, 77
metric system, 94
Metro station, Washington, D.C.
    vaulting in, *89*, 92
Metropolitan Opera House
    of Lincoln Center, *11*, 12, 16, 30
Michelangelo, Buonarotti, 92
    Campidoglio of, *7*, *8*, *10*, 12, *13*
    Capital of, 64, 142
    giant order of, 34, 156
Miës van der Rohe, Ludwig
    Cartesian skyscrapers of, 24–25
    classical expression of, 92
    collages of, 115
    conservative modernism and, 111
    construction materials and, 65
    façade articulation by, 57

Illinois Institute of Technology by, *130*, *131*, 134
Main Post Office by, 35, *36*, 37, *38*, 111
planning grids and, 94
Seagram Building by, 58, *59*, 60, 111
minimalism, 37
Mizner, Addison
    Palm Beach house design by, *132–133*, 136
modern
    classical vs., 2–3
    definition of, 2
modern architecture. *See also* modernism
    aesthetic choices in, 21
    balance of force in, 83, *84*, *85*, 86
    building scale in, 21
    building techniques in, 152
    circulation in, 54
    climate influence on, 25
    concept of shelter in, 117, *118–119*
    construction material evolution and, 25
    coordination of, 53–54
    coordination of systems in, 31–32
    disjuncture in, 6, 53, 65, 114, 139, 142, 154
    dissociation in, 53, 121–122
    dynamic balance in, 53, 83, 104, 124
    dynamic form of, 122
    economic forces in, 19–21
    enclosure in, 23–25, 67–77, 144
    environment in, 23, 24
    equivalency in, 6, 34–35, 124, 139
    glass in, 7, 12
    independent space and, 26–27
    interior-exterior material coordination in, 148–149
    lightness of, 27, 152
    structural support and, 121–122
    motion and, 83, *84*, *85*, 86
    movement through, 54
    multiple grid in, 154, *155*
    outside-inside distinction in, 117, 120
    parts vs. system in, 29
    perception in, 53, 144, 148
    vs. materiality, 149, 152
    perception of nature and, 47
    plan of, 154, *155*
    planar quality of, 152

planning unit in, 136
relationship to street of, 125
social mobility and, 26
social-economic forces in esthetics vs., 21
spatial organization in, 20, 21–27, 60, 66–67. *See also* space
spatial-structural interaction in, 114
subject matter of, 120
support and space in, 27
symmetry in, 46
tactility in, 66
technology and, 58
transparency in, 27, 37, 149
two-dimensional design and, 67
vaulted space in, 92
walls in, 30
modern motifs
    classical motifs combined with, 2, 3
Modern Movement
    architect's intention and, 16, 18
    codification of, 7
    International Style and, 111
    Lincoln Center and, 7
modernism. *See also* modern architecture
    classical ideal in, 4, 111
    classicism vs., 5, 16, 18
    conflict in, 115
    contrast in, 60
    definition of, 102–114
    cultural development and, 105–114
    dynamic action and, 104
    democracy and, 5–6, 19, 64
    denial of classicism in, 60, 65, 142
    determinants of, 5
    development of, 19–21
    social and cultural conditions in, 5–7
    failure of, 111, 114
    function of, 3–4
    "heroic" period of, 4
    hierarchical vs. heterarchical systems in, 139, 142
    history and, 19–64
    inclusiveness in, 6, 23, 124
    inner-outer relation in, 16
    intellectualization of culture and, 3, 20
    organizing principle of, 4–5
    relating function in, 22
    social forces in, 19–21
    tenets of, 20

themed artifact and, 4
theory of, 7
traditional culture and, 6
uncertainty in, 104–105
as utopian, 20
modularity
    of building unit, 57, 156
    of churches, 60, *61*, *62*, 64
    classical structure of, 98, 154, 156
    concept of space and, 67
    construction techniques and, 156
    cultural influences on, 134–136
    expression of, 156
    façade articulation in, 54, *55*, *56*, 57
    form and, 154, 156–158
    of functional unit, 57–58, 156, 158
    geometry in, 86, *87*
    of government buildings, *63*, 64
    individual space in, *135*, 136
    modern structure of, 98, 100, 156
    as planning unit, 42, 54–57
    of Seagram Building, 58, *59*, 60
    of structural bay, 57
    as subdivided block, 134
    technology and, 98, *99*, 100
Modulor system of measurement and proportion, 27, 46, 121
monuments
    private house vs., 29
Moretti, Luigi
    Casa del Girasole by, *141*
Morrill Act (1862)
    campus planning and, 129
Morris, William, 46
Morse and Stiles Colleges
    at Yale University, 115, *116*
    street plan and, 125, 128
movement, 54
multiculturalism
    disjuncture and, 114
Municipal Building, New York, 92
Museum of Modern Art, New York
    1930 exhibition at, 7
    urban renewal and, 14
music
    classicism and, 107

nature
    architectural relation to, 24
    classical vs. modern perception of, 47
    force and movement in, 103
    mathematical basis of, 102

INDEX

neoclassicism, 5, 34
   building materials and, 88
   concept of space in, 21
New York, New York
   modern architecture development and, 20–21
New York State Theater
   of Lincoln Center, *9*, *13*
New York Telephone Company Building, *112*
Nolli plan of Rome, 125, *128*
Norberg-Schulz, Christian, 66, 114

office buildings
   classical styles in, 43
   as functional unit, 57
Old Colony Railroad Station, North Easton, Mass., 67, *68*, 70
Old Meeting House, Lancaster, Mass., 60, *61*, *62*
Olmsted, Frederick Law, 42
On Growth and Form, 42, 66, 83, 103
On Growth and Function, 104
On the Origin of Species, 66, 125
Oratorio of S. Filippo Neri, Rome, 102, *106*
organic architecture, 66
organization
   axiality and, 128
   Cartesian, 43
   city grid system in, 94, *95–97*, 98
   classical, 34, 37, 42, 125, 154
   modern, 34, 42, 125, 154, *155*
   of streets, 125, *126*, *127*, 128
   of university campus, 129, *130*, *131*, 134
   zoning and, 128
orientation
   classical vs. modern, 46–47, 98
ornamentation
   abstraction vs., 88
outside-inside distinction
   building technology and, 25, 77–78
   classical standard and, 25, 77–78, 148
   in modern churches, 117, 120
   modern interpretation of, 148
   royalty and, 117
   structural integrity and, 78
Owings and Merrill
   Inland Steel Building by, *135*, 136
ownership
   occupancy vs., 120

Oxford University, England
   tutorial system of, 134

painting
   modern architecture and, 30
Palace of Fine Arts, San Francisco, *140*
palaces
   hierarchical order of, 117, 120
Palazzo dei Senatori
   of Campidoglio, *10*
Palazzo Nuovo
   of Campidoglio, *8*, *14*
Palladio, Andrea
   architectural drawings of, 120
   Church of S. Giorgio Magiore by, *138*
   classical principles of, 34
   exterior-interior articulation by, 139
   Il Redentore by, *75*
   neoclassical architecture and, 64
   primary-secondary spaces and, 22
   wall articulation by, 27, 69
Palm Beach, Florida
   Addison Mizner designs in, *132–133*, 136
Pan-Pacific Auditorium, Los Angeles, 117, *118–119*
Pantheon, Rome
   University of Virginia plan and, 129
paper making
   industrialization of architectural drawings and, 88
Park Avenue, New York
   railroad development and, 43, 60
Pei, I. M.
   Louvre and, 53
Penn Mutual Life Building, Philadelphia, 125, *126*
Penn Station, New York, 35
   African American theater displacement by, 14
   demolition of, 23
   Hellenic Doric order of, 104
Pennsylvania Railroad
   James J. Farley Post Office and, 37
perception
   in modern architecture, 53–54, 66–67, 144, 149, 152
   of nature, 47
phenomenal transparency, 47
Philharmonic Hall
   of Lincoln Center, 12, 14, *14*

physics
   technological effects of, 66
planning unit
   individual space multiplied in, *132–133*, 134, *135*, 136
plasticity
   of building construction, 29–30
   in classical vs. modern architecture, 152
   cultural change and, 122, 124
   form and, 152
   tactile vs. visual, 122, 124
   technologic advances and, 92
political system
   centralized
      classical image in, 139
   two-party
      as modernist expression, 142
Polk, Willis
   Hallidie Building by, *76*
polyarchy
   hierarchy vs., 124
post-modernism, 2
   classicism and, 114
Prairie houses
   of Frank Lloyd Wright, 25, 98, 124
privacy
   modern house and, 115, 117
procession, 54
   axiality and, 128
   classical, 148
proportion
   classical application of, 43, 46, 102–103, 120–121
   force and, 103–104
   force in, 104
   modern application of, 46
   in site planning, 43

railroad coaches
   motion expression and, *85*, 86
railroad stations
   classical vs. modern elements of, 128
railroads
   influence on street plans of, 128
   site planning and, 43
Rankine & Kellog
   U.S. Post Office, Philadelphia by, 37, *39*
realism, 30
reality
   in modernism, 4

rectangular grid
   in city planning, 42
rectilinear grid
   abstraction of, 125
reinforced concrete
   classical construction ideals and, 69
   column shape and, 100
   concept of weight and, 69
religion
   personalization of, 137
religious art
   human naturalistic depiction in, 139
Renaissance architecture, 142
   structural system interplay in, 64
Renaissance ideal, 139
Rice University, Louisiana
   School of Architecture at, *153*
Richard Hughes Justice Complex, Trenton, New Jersey, 69, *74*
Richards Medical Laboratories, University of Pennsylvania, *143*
Richardson, Henry Hobson
   Ames Library by, *90*, *91*, 92
   architectural style of, 105
   Crane Memorial Library by, 92, *93*
Rittenhouse Square, Philadelphia
   classical elements in, 6, *6*
Rockefeller Center, New York
   classical composition of, 14
   International Style planning of, 60
   as urban renewal, 14
Roman civilization
   Greek principles in, 139
   understanding vs. experiencing of, 3
Romanesque revival, 5
Rome
   Capital at, 12
   papal reconstruction of, 142
rooms
   classical arrangement of, 53
Rossellino, Bernardo, 7
Rossi, Aldo, 3, 23, 66
Rowe, Colin, 47, 144, 148
royalty
   classical architecture and, 25–26
Rudolph, Paul, 78
   Boston Government Service Center by, 69, *73*
   modularity and, 156
Rue de Rivoli, Paris, 154
Ruskin, John, 21, 26, 53, 77–78, 83, 148, 156

INDEX

Saarinen, Eero, 16, 78
    CBS Building by, 27, *28*, 122
    Dulles Airport by, 77, *79*
    Morse and Stiles Colleges by, 115, *116*
    Vivian Beaumont Theater, Lincoln Center by, *15*, 16
sacred places. *See also* churches
    equivalence vs. hierarchy in, 60–64
    in Greek civilization, 137, *139*
Safdie, Moshe
    Habitat, Montreal by, 156
School of Architecture, Rice University, *153*
science
    classicism and, 107
    concept of space and, 142, 144
Scott-Brown, Denise, 78
screens
    sliding, 149
    in spatial independence, 144, 148
Seagram Building, New York, 65, 111
    modern vs. classical content of, 58, *59*, 60
    plasticity of, 152
    street plan and, 125
sealants, 92
Seven Lamps of Architecture, The, 26, 53, 77–78, 83, 148
Sever Hall, Harvard University, 105
shapes
    structure and, 149
shelter
    modernist concept of, 117, *118–119*
site planning
    Cartesian organization in, 43
    commercial development in, 94, *96–97*
    incremental grid in, 94
    industrialization and, 42
    proportion in, 43, 46
    transportation and, 43, 94, *95*, 125, *126*, *127*, 128
    zoning regulations and, 42, 94, 98, 128
Sixtus V
    plan of Rome by, 128
Skidmore, Owings and Merrill
    Lever House by, *157*
    U. S. Steel Building by, 78, *82*

skyscrapers, 24–25
    design evolution of, 122
    height of, 42, 122
    lightness of, 27
Slutzky, Robert, 47, 144, 148
social status
    proportion and, 120–121
society
    general vs. specialized knowledge and, 19
    individual within, 19, 31
Society Hill, Philadelphia, *48*
solid and void, 66
    building technology and, 83, 86
    classical concept of, 21, 83, 121–122, 148
    spatial concepts and, 26–27, 144
    wind pressure and, 83, 86
space
    abstraction of, 21–22
    air circulation and, 83
    architectural history and, 26–27
    central, 42
    classical concept of, 66
        enclosure in, 144
        modern concept vs., 21–27
        organization of, 37, 42
        solid and void in, 21, 148
    as composite of elements
        architectural drawings and, 88
    cultural change and, 114–120
    disjunctured expression of, 142, 144
    enclosure in, 22–25, 67–77, 144, 148. *See also* enclosure
    as field of action, 21
    form and, 142–149
    functional zones and, 47
    independent, 20, 26
        screens in, 144, 148
    layering of, 149
    mental reconstruction of, 66–67
    modern concept of, 20, 60, 66–67, 120
        classical concept vs., 21–27
    outside-inside distinction in, 148–149
    phenomenal transparency of, 47
    plasticity and, 122, *123*, 124
    science and, 142, 144
    solid and void in, 26–27, 144
    and support, 27

    technology and, 66–86
    virtual, 67, *123*, 124, 144
    wind pressure and, 83
Space, Time and Architecture: the Growth of a New Tradition, 88
spirituality
    spatial representation of, 114
square
    in classical architecture, 43, 46
St. Peter's, Rome, 46
states
    incremental grid for, 94
steel construction
    concept of weight and, 69
steel structural bay, 100
Stirling, James
    School of Architecture, Rice University by, *153*
street planning
    Cartesian organization in, *40–41*, 43
    classical façade and, 154
    commercial development in, 94, *95–97*, 98
    incremental grid in, 94
    industrialization in, 42
    modern buildings and, 154
    proportion in, 43, 46
    railroads in, 128
    transportation and, 43, 125, *126*, 127
    zoning in, 128
structural bay
    classical, 57, 125
    detailing of, 35
    modern, 57
    as modular element, 57, 98, 100, 154, 156
    repetition of, 156
    steel/reinforced concrete, 100
structure
    expression of, 77–78
Stubbins, Hugh
    Citicorp Center by, *127*
Sullivan, Louis
    Carson Pirie Scott department store by, 57
    classical ideal and, 158
    Columbian Exposition of 1893 and, 105
    Condit Building by, *158*
Summerson, John, 3–4, 92, 94, 105
support
    classical vs. modern concept of, 27

Supreme Court of the United States, 69
Supreme Courtroom of New Jersey, 69
surface
    modern vs. classical view of, 152
Sydney Opera House, Australia, 16, *17*, 18
symbolism
    classicism and, 115
symmetry, 124
    axiality and, 46
    dynamic balance and, 53

tactility, 35, 66, 121
tatami mat
    Frank Lloyd Wright and, 117
    modular design and, 42
Technical University, Otaniemi, Finland, 154, *155*
technology, 65–100
    architectural change from, 139
    architectural drawings and, 88
    architectural style and, 12
    coordination of systems and, 92, 94
    enclosure and, 67–77
    frames and, 69, *75*, 77
    geometry and, 86–94
    independence of building systems and, 65
    membranes and, 77, *79*
    in modernism, 58
    modularity and, 98, *99*, 100
    organization and, 94–98
    orientation and, 98
    plasticity and, 92
    site planning and, 94, *95–97*, 98
    solid and void and, 83
    space and, 66–86
    urban services and, 98
    walls and, 67, 69
    weight and, 67, 69
tectonics, 92, 121–122, 152
    of classical architecture, 148
temple
    in classical architecture, 137, *138*
tent
    as framed architecture, 77
    as membrane, 77
Terrangni, Giuseppe, 46
theater
    African American, 14

INDEX

Thomas Hocklin House, Philadelphia, 144, *146*
Thompson, D'Arcy Wentworth, 42, 66, 83, 103, 104
three-dimensional grid, 24
three-dimensions
  two-dimensional expression of, 122
Times Square, New York, 3
transparency
  in modern architecture, 37, 149
"Transparency, Literal and Phenomenal," 144, 148
transportation
  city planning and, 43, 94
  street planning and, 125, 128
triangulation, 86, *87*
trusses
  triangulation of, 86, *87*

U. S. Steel Building, New York, 78, *82*
Unité d'Habitation, Marseilles, 98, 100, 125
Unity Temple, Oak Park, Ill., 46
universities
  American vs. European, 129, 134
  architectural design of, 129–134
University Library, Otaniemi, Finland, 99
University of Pennsylvania, Philadelphia
  Library at, *123*, 124
  Richards Medical Laboratories at, *143*, 144
University of Virginia, Charlottesville
  planning of, 129
urban renewal
  neighborhood transformation through, 14
  neoclassicism and, 5

urban services, 98
U.S. Post Office, Philadelphia, 37, *39*
Utzon, Jörn, 16, *17*, 78

Vanbrugh, John, 120
vaulting
  in ancient architecture, 88
  in modern architecture, 92
  modularity in, 156
  space and, 20
ventilation
  concept of space and, 83
Ventura, Calif.
  development of, *96–97*
Venturi, Robert, 3, 78
Versailles
  hierarchical plan of, 117
Versailles, France, 98
view
  control of, 47, 53
Villa Stein, Garches, 47
Viollet-le-Duc, 156
virtual space, 67, *123*, 124, 144
Vivian Beaumont Repertory Theater, Lincoln Center, *15*, 16
void
  and solid. See solid and void
Voorhees, Gmelin & Walker
  New York Telephone Company Building by, *112*
voussoirs, 88, 92

Walker, Ralph
  skyscrapers of, 111, *112*, *113*
walls
  classical, 27, 30, 149
  exterior vs. interior, 122
  glass, 77

layering systems in, 149
meaning of, 27
modern, 30
as object in space, 148
plasticity of, 29–30
as screening elements, 144
spatial independence and, 115
as supports, 67, 69
vs. enclosure, 78
Washington, D. C.
  orientation of, 98
  street planning of, 94
  zoning and, 128
Washington Monument, Washington, D.C., 34–35
weight
  in classical architecture, 83
  size and scale and, 67, 69
Weissenhof Exhibition of 1927, Stuttgart, 111
Western architecture
  central space in, 37, 42
  classical tradition of, 5
  climate and, 25
Western culture
  separated systems in, 142
Wharton, Edith, 22, 30, 43, 46, 101, 102, 104, 117, 121, 124
white space, 30
Williamsburg, Va.
  themed artifact and, 4
wind pressure
  concept of space and, 83
work
  industrialization and, 24–25
workplace
  as building type, 24
workstation
  hierarchical, 156, 158

World War I
  modern design and, 111
World's Fair, New York (1939), 35
Wright, Frank Lloyd
  axiality and, 46
  Beth Sholom Synagogue by, 117
  disjuncture and, 142
  dissociation and, 53
  enclosure and, 22, 67
  Florida Southern College by, 129, 134, 154
  frontality and, 98
  "In the Cause of Architecture" by, 102
  interior-exterior coordination by, 148
  Japanese influence on, 107, 111, 117
  modernism and, 5
  modular design principles of, 42
  organic architecture and, 66
  plasticity and, 152
  Prairie houses of, 25, 98, 124
  tent prototypes of, 77
  Usonian houses of, 98, 154
Wurdeman & Becket
  Pan-Pacific Auditorium of, *118–119*

Yale University, New Haven, Conn.
  Davenport College at, 78, *80–81*
  Gothic Revival and, 78, *80–81*
  Morse and Stiles Colleges at, 115, *116*, 125, 128
  planning of, 129

zoning, 128
  site planning and, 5, 42, 94, 98, 128